FIRST STEP
中文起步

The Princeton Language Program: Modern Chinese

Princeton University Press is proud to publish the Princeton Language Program in Modern Chinese. Based on courses taught through Princeton University Department of East Asian Studies and the Princeton in Beijing Program, this comprehensive series is designed for university students who wish to learn or improve upon their knowledge of Mandarin Chinese.

Students begin with *First Step, Chinese Primer,* or *Oh, China!* depending on their previous exposure to the language. After the first year, any combination of texts at a given level can be used. While all of the intermediate and advanced texts focus on modern life in China, and especially on the media, texts marked with an asterisk (*) in the chart below compare China to the United States and are particularly appropriate for American students.

PROGRAM OVERVIEW

First Year	Second Year	Third Year	Advanced
First Step	*A New China*	*A Kaleidoscope of China*	*Anything Goes*
Chinese Primer (For beginners with no previous knowledge of Chinese)	*A Trip to China*	*All Things Considered*	*China's Own Critics*
Oh, China! (For students who speak and understand some Chinese, especially "heritage" students who speak the language at home)	*An Intermediate Reader of Modern Chinese**	*Newspaper Readings**	*China's Peril and Promise*
			Literature and Society
			Readings in Contemporary Chinese Cinema

FIRST STEP

中文起步

An Elementary Reader for Modern Chinese

Chih-p'ing Chou
Jing Wang
Jun Lei

PRINCETON UNIVERSITY PRESS
Princeton and Oxford

Published by Princeton University Press, 41 William Street, Princeton, New Jersey 08540
In the United Kingdom: Princeton University Press, 6 Oxford Street, Woodstock, Oxfordshire OX20 1TW

press.princeton.edu

The Chinese character stroke diagrams and worksheets in the *First Step* workbook are licensed
from the website http://www.ArchChinese.com, developed by Arch Learning Services

ISBN 978-0-691-15420-6

Library of Congress Control Number: 2013936222
British Library Cataloging-in-Publication Data is available

This book has been composed in Times Pinyin and Avenir
Printed on acid-free paper. ∞
Printed in the United States of America

10 9 8 7 6 5 4 3 2 1

CONTENTS

A：我不喜歡上海菜，因為上海菜太甜了。

B：北京烤鴨太油了，上海菜太甜了，今天我們在紐約吃什麼？

A：這是你第一次來紐約，我們吃紐約牛排吧！

B：好！

Yìzhāng Zhàopiàn (A Picture)

Pinyin Text

(A—Zhāng Sān, B—Dīng Yī)

A: Xiǎo Dīng, qiángshang yǒu yìzhāng zhàopiàn, zhàopiàn shang shì shéi?

B: Zhàopiàn shang shì wǒde jiārén.

A: Nǎyíge shì nǐ bàba?

B: Zhōngjiān de nèige shì wǒ bàba.

A: Māma ne?

B: Māma zài bàba de zuǒbiānr. Bàba de yòubiānr shì gēge.

A: Nǐ yǒuméiyǒu dìdi?

B: Wǒ yǒu yíge dìdi.

A: Dìdi zài nǎr?

English Translation

(A—Zhang San, B—Ding Yi)

A: Xiao Ding, there is a picture on the wall. Who are in the picture?

B: The picture is of my family.

A: Which one is your father?

B: The one in the middle is my father.

A: And your mother?

B: My mom is to my dad's left. To my father's right is my older brother.

A: Do you have any younger brothers?

B: I have one younger brother.

A: Where is your younger brother?

照片		zhàopiàn	n.	photograph, picture
墙	墙	qiáng	n.	wall
家		jiā	n.	home; family
家人		jiārén	n.	family member
爸爸		bàba	n.	father, dad
中间	中間	zhōngjiān	n.	middle, center
妈妈	媽媽	māma	n.	mother
呢		ne	part.	to make a follow-up question

第五课 一张照片

（A——张三，B——丁一）

A：小丁，墙上有一张照片，照片上是谁？

B：照片上是我的家人。

A：哪一个是你爸爸？

B：中间的那个是我爸爸。

A：妈妈呢？

B：妈妈在爸爸的左边儿。爸爸的右边儿是哥哥。

A：你有没有弟弟？

B：我有一个弟弟。

A：弟弟在哪儿？

左边(儿)	左邊(兒)	zuǒbiān(r)	n.	left side
右边(儿)	右邊(兒)	yòubiān(r)	n.	right side
哥哥		gēge	n.	older brother
弟弟		dìdi	n.	younger brother

B: Dìdi zài gēge de hòubiānr. wǒ zài dìdi hé jiějie de zhōngjiān. Wǒ gēge hěn ǎi, dìdi hěn gāo.

A: Nǐ dìdi duōdà?

B: Wǒ dìdi shísì suì. Gēge suīrán bǐ dìdi dà liǎngsuì, kěshì méiyǒu dìdi nènme gāo. Dìdi bǐ wǒ gāo, yě bǐ gēge gāo. Tā shì wǒmen jiā zuìgāo de.

A: Nǐ jiějie hòubiān de nèige nánde shì shéi?

B: Tā shì wǒ jiějie de xiānsheng.

A: Nǐ jiějie jiéhūn le, yǒu háizi ma?

B: Tā suīrán jiéhūn le, kěshì hái méiyǒu háizi.

B: My younger brother is behind my older brother. I am in between my younger brother and older sister. My older brother is short, and my younger brother is tall.

A: How old is your younger brother?

B: My younger brother is fourteen years old. Although my older brother is two years older than my younger brother, he is not as tall as my younger brother. My younger brother is taller than me and taller than my older brother too. He is the tallest in our family.

A: Who is that man behind your older sister?

B: He is my older sister's husband.

A: Your older sister is married. Does she have children?

B: Although she is married, she doesn't have any children yet.

后边(儿) 後邊(兒)	hòubiān(r)	prep.	back, behind
姐姐	jiějie	n.	older sister
矮	ǎi	adj.	short (to describe height)
高	gāo	adj.	tall; high
多大	duō dà	phrase	how old?
比	bǐ	prep./v.	used in comparison; to compare

B：弟弟在哥哥的后边儿。我在弟弟和姐姐的中间。我哥哥很矮，弟弟很高。

A：你弟弟多大？

B：我弟弟14岁。哥哥虽然比弟弟大两岁，可是没有弟弟那么高。弟弟比我高，也比哥哥高。他是我们家最高的。

A：你姐姐后边儿的那个男的是谁？

B：他是我姐姐的先生。

A：你姐姐结婚了，有孩子吗？

B：她虽然结婚了，可是还没有孩子。

大		dà	adj.	old in age; big in size
岁	歲	suì	n.	age
那么	那麼	nènme	adv.	so (+ adj./adv.)
男的		nánde	n.	man, male
先生		xiānsheng	n.	husband; mister, gentleman
结婚	結婚	jiéhūn	v.	to get married; to marry
她		tā	pron.	she; her
还 + negative	還	hái	adv.	not yet
孩子		háizi	n.	child, kid

A: Nǐ jiějie pángbiānr de nèige nǚháizi shì shéi?

B: Tā shì wǒ mèimei. Mèimei suīrán bǐ jiějie xiǎo sìsuì, kěshì tā hé jiějie yíyàng gāo.

A: Nǐ mèimei zhēn piàoliang.

B: Wǒ mèimei búdàn piàoliang, érqiě cōngming.

A: Tā yǒu nán péngyou ma?

B: Tā hái méiyǒu nán péngyou.

A: Tàihǎole! Wǒ míngtiān qǐngtā hē kāfēi.

B: Kěshì … kěshì … tā bǐ nǐ gāodeduō, yě bǐ nǐ cōngming.

A: Who is that girl next to your older sister?

B: She is my younger sister. Although my younger sister is four years younger than my older sister, she is as tall as my older sister.

A: Your younger sister is really pretty.

B: Not only is my younger sister pretty, but she is also smart.

A: Does she have a boyfriend?

B: She doesn't have a boyfriend yet.

A: Excellent! Tomorrow I will invite her to drink coffee.

B: However … she is much taller than you, and she is smarter than you too.

女		nǚ	adj./n.	female; woman
女孩子		nǚ háizi	n.	girl
妹妹		mèimei	n.	younger sister
小		xiǎo	adj.	young in age, small in size
一样	一樣	yíyàng	adv.	the same

A：你姐姐旁边儿的那个女孩子是谁？

B：她是我妹妹。妹妹虽然比姐姐小四岁，可是她和姐姐一样高。

A：你妹妹真漂亮。

B：我妹妹不但漂亮，而且聪明。

A：她有男朋友吗？

B：她还没有男朋友。

A：太好了！我明天请她喝咖啡。

B：可是……可是……她比你高得多，也比你聪明。

真		zhēn	adv.	really
不但……而且		búdàn … érqiě	…conj.	not only … but also …
聪明	聰明	cōngming	adj.	clever, smart
男朋友		nán péngyou	n.	boyfriend
明天		míngtiān	n.	tomorrow
得		de	part.	complement marker

语法 Grammar Notes

1. Determinative and Question Word: 哪 (which)

哪, as a determinative, functions in the same way as 这 (this) and 那 (that).

哪本书	nǎ běn shū	which book
哪两个中国字	nǎ liǎngge zhōngguózì	which two Chinese characters

▶ 哪一个是你爸爸？

Nǎyíge shì nǐ bàba?

Which one is your father?

In the above example, two things need to be pointed out:

a. The possessive 的 can be omitted when the possessor is a personal pronoun and the possessed are people who have a close relationship with the possessor, such as parents or siblings; therefore, both 你的爸爸 and 你爸爸 are correct expressions; but if the combination is used as a modifier, 的 is often omitted to avoid redundancy; therefore, 我妈妈的学生 is preferred to 我的妈妈的学生.

b. 哪 is a question word. When forming a question, replace the determinative in the answer (usually 这 or 那) with 哪 and keep the original sentence order.

Q: 哪本书是你的(书)？

Nǎ běn shū shì nǐde (shū)?

Which book is yours?

A: 这本书是我的(书)。

Zhèi běn shū shì wǒde (shū).

This book is mine.

2. Place Words

In Lesson 2, we discussed some location words: 上头 (on top of), 下头 (under/below), and 旁边儿 (beside). In this lesson, some new location words from the same category are added: 中间 (middle, center), 左边儿 (left side), 右边儿 (right side), 后边儿 (back side, behind). To point out the relative location of A in reference to B, use the following pattern:

A在B的左边儿 / 右边儿 / 后边儿

A在B和C的中间 (A is between B and C)

▶ 我在弟弟和姐姐的中间。

Wǒ zài dìdi hé jiějie de zhōngjiān.

I am between my younger brother and older sister.

58

Place words can be used as modifiers.

> ▶ 中间的那个是我爸爸。
> Zhōngjiān de nèige shì wǒ bàba.
> The one in the middle is my father.

中间 in this sentence is used as a modifier for 那个(人) (that (person)).

3. Particle 呢

In this lesson, the particle 呢 comes directly after a word or phrase to form a follow-up question. It is usually translated into English as "how about … ?" The content of the question and the context are understood. The purpose of the question is to get further information about the topic.

> ▶ 妈妈呢？
> Māma ne?
> How about your mother?

> 你不喜欢吃汉堡包。纽约牛排呢？
> Nǐ bù xǐhuān chī hànbǎobāo. Niǔyuē niúpái ne?
> You don't like to eat hamburgers. How about the New York steak?

4. Conjunction 和 (and)

和 is used to connect two words or phrases of the same or similar structure and grammatical function. It is not completely equivalent to "and" in English, which can connect two sentences, such as "I would like to meet your younger sister, and invite her to have a cup of coffee." However, in Chinese, 和 can never connect two sentences. A typical mistake that English-speaking students make is to overuse 和 in Chinese.

> 中文书和英文书都是老师的。
> Zhōngwén shū hé Yīngwén shū dōushì lǎoshī de.
> Both the Chinese book and the English book are the teacher's.

> 我去北京学中文和工作。
> Wǒ qù Běijīng xué Zhōngwén hé gōngzuò.
> I will go to Beijing to study Chinese and to work.

5. Comparison

To compare A and B, use the following pattern:

Positive form: 　　A 比 B + adj. A is more ... than B
　　　　　　　　　A 比 B + adj. + complement

The positive form can be extended by adding complements after the adjective. The complements can be in the form of degree and amount. For example:

▶ 她比你高得多。

Tā bǐ nǐ gāodeduō.

She is much taller than you.

In the above example, following the main adjective 高 is a complement to indicate the degree of the comparison (i.e., much taller). The complement consists of two elements: 得 (verb/adjective complement marker) and an adjective. In addition to 多, some other adjectives can be used as a complement in a comparison sentence. But for now, just remember the following pattern:

A 比 B adj. 得多　　　(A is much more ... than B)

Number or amount can also be used as a complement. For example,

E 哥哥比弟弟大两岁。　　　Gēge bǐ dìdi dà liǎngsuì.

Older brother is two years older than younger brother.

妹妹比姐姐小四岁。

Mèimei bǐ jiějie xiǎo sìsuì.

Younger sister is four years younger than older sister.

Negative form: 　　A 没有 B + (那么) adj.　　A is not as ... as B

▶ 哥哥没有弟弟那么高。

Gēge méiyǒu dìdi nènme gāo.

Older brother is not as tall as younger brother.

A 和 B 一样 + adj.　　A is the same ... as B

▶ 她和姐姐一样高。

Tā hé jiějie yíyàng gāo.

She is as tall as older sister.

纽约牛排和北京烤鸭一样好吃。

Niǔyuē niúpái hé Běijīng kǎoyā yíyàng hǎochī.

New York steak is as delicious as Beijing roast duck.

6. 最 + adj. (the most)

In Lesson 4, we have learned 最喜欢 (to like the most). In addition to combining with emotion verbs such as 喜欢, 最 is often followed by adjectives to indicate the highest level.

最好	zuìhǎo	the best
最高	zuìgāo	the tallest
最聪明	zuìcōngming	the smartest
最漂亮	zuìpiàoliang	the most beautiful

Scope words can be put in front of the 最 phrase:

▶ 他是我们家最高的。
Tāshì wǒmen jiā zuìgāo de.
He is the tallest one in our family.

我妹妹是我们家最聪明的。
Wǒ mèimei shì wǒmen jiā zuì cōngming de.
My younger sister is the smartest one in our family.

7. Asking about One's Age

There are two common ways to ask about one's age:

Subject 多大(了)?
Subject 几岁(了)?

The first one is a question form that can be used generally to ask for anyone's age. The second form is usually used for children. It can also be used by a senior person to ask for the age of a junior person.

8. Particle 了

In this lesson, the particle 了 appears at the end of the verb phrase 结婚. It indicates that the action of the subject, that is, to get married, has been completed. When 了 appears after a verb, it indicates completion of an action. Other functions of 了 will be introduced in later lessons.

▶ 你姐姐结婚了。
Nǐ jiějiě jiéhūn le.
Your older sister is married.

To negate a sentence with 了, use **没有 + verb.**

你姐姐没有结婚。
Nǐ jiějie méiyǒu jiéhūn.
Your older sister is not married.

9. 还 adv. (still)

▶ 她虽然结婚了，可是还没有孩子。

Tā suīrán jiéhūn le, kěshì hái méi yǒu háizi.

Although she is married, she has no children yet.

▶ 她还没有男朋友。

Tā hái méiyou nán péngyou.

She doesn't have a boyfriend yet.

他还没有结婚。

Tā hái méi jiéhūn.

He is not married yet.

Note: In the above examples, 没有 has different meanings and grammatical functions. In 没有孩子 and 没有男朋友, 没有 (do not have) is the negative form of the concrete verb 有 (to have), however, in 没有结婚 (is not married/did not get married), 没有 negates the verb 结婚.

10. 不但……而且…… (not only ... but also ...)

Subject 不但 V.P.1/adj.1, 而且 V.P. 2/adj.2

▶ 我的妹妹不但漂亮，而且聪明。

Wǒde mèimei búdàn piàoliang, érqiě cōngming.

Not only is my younger sister pretty, but she is also smart.

我不但有中文书，而且有英文书。

Wǒ búdàn yǒu Zhōngwén shū, érqiě yǒu Yīngwén shū.

I not only have Chinese books, but also have English books.

The elements after 不但/而且 must talk about things in the same category or be closely related or express meaning in the same direction, that is, both are positive or both are negative. 而且 can be used without a preceding 不但 clause. In this case, 而且 simply means "in addition, moreover."

Cultural Notes

Family Members

家人

Since the implementation of the "One Child Policy" in the late 1970s, most Chinese families in urban areas have only one child. However, to have a big family, as expressed in the Chinese phrase sìshì tóngtáng 四世同堂 (four generations in the same household), is considered a great blessing in traditional Chinese society. Associated with this concept and with the existence of many family members on both sides of a family, there are different terms for various relatives. The following table lists titles that are still frequently used for one's close relatives.

On father's side			On mother's side		
爸爸	bàba	father	妈妈	māma	mother
爷爷	yéye	grandfather	姥爷	lǎoye	grandfather
奶奶	nǎinai	grandmother	姥姥	lǎolao	grandmother
叔叔	shūshu	uncle	舅舅	jiùjiu	uncle
婶婶	shěnshen	aunt-in-law	舅妈	jiùmā	aunt-in-law
姑姑	gūgu	aunt	(阿)姨	(ā)yí	aunt
姑父	gūfu	uncle-in-law	姨父	yífu	uncle-in-law
堂哥	tánggē	older cousin (boy)	表哥	biǎogē	older cousin (boy)
堂弟	tángdì	younger cousin (boy)	表弟	biǎodì	younger cousin (boy)
堂姐	tángjiě	older cousin (girl)	表姐	biǎojiě	older cousin (girl)
堂妹	tángmèi	younger cousin (girl)	表妹	biǎomèi	younger cousin (girl)

Traditional Character Text

一張照片

（A——張三，B——丁一）

A：小丁，墙上有一張照片，照片上是誰？

B：照片上是我的家人。

A：哪一個是你爸爸？

B：中間的那個是我爸爸。

A：媽媽呢？

B：媽媽在爸爸的左邊兒。爸爸的右邊兒是哥哥。

A：你有沒有弟弟？

B：我有一個弟弟。

A：弟弟在哪兒？

B：弟弟在哥哥的后邊兒。我在弟弟和姐姐的中間。我哥哥很矮，弟弟很高。

A：你弟弟多大？

B：我弟弟14歲。哥哥雖然比弟弟大兩歲，可是沒有弟弟那麼高。弟弟比我高，也比哥哥高。他是我們家最高的。

A：你姐姐后邊兒的那個男的是誰？

B：他是我姐姐的先生。

A：你姐姐結婚了，有孩子嗎？

B：她雖然結婚了，可是還沒有孩子。

A：你姐姐旁邊兒的那個女孩子是誰？

B：她是我妹妹。妹妹雖然比姐姐小四歲，可是她和姐姐一樣高。

A：你妹妹真漂亮。

B：我妹妹不但漂亮，而且聰明。

A：她有男朋友嗎？

B：她還沒有男朋友。

A：太好了！我明天請她喝咖啡。

B：可是……可是……她比你高得多，也比你聰明。

6 Wǒde Liǎngge Péngyou (My Two Friends)

Pinyin Text

(A—Dīng Yī, B—Zhāng Sān)

A: Nǐ yǒu Zhōngguó péngyou ma?

B: Wǒ méiyǒu Zhōngguó péngyou, kěshì, wǒ yǒu liǎngge zài Zhōngguó de péngyou.

A: Tāmen zài nǎr a?

B: Yíge zài Běijīng, yíge zài Shànghǎi.

A: Tāmen huìbúhuì shuō Zhōngguóhuà?

B: Zài Běijīng de péngyou shì Měiguó rén, huì shuō yìdiǎnr Zhōngwén, kěshì shuōde bùhǎo. Zài Shànghǎi de péngyou shì Rìběn rén, tā búdàn huì shuō Zhōngguó huà, érqiě huì xiě Zhōngguó zì.

A: Nǐ gēn tāmen shuō shénme huà?

English Translation

(A—Ding Yi, B—Zhang San)

A: Do you have Chinese friends?

B: I don't have any Chinese friends, but I have two friends in China.

A: Where are they?

B: One is in Beijing, and one is in Shanghai.

A: Can they speak Chinese?

B: The friend in Beijing is an American. He can speak a little Chinese, but he speaks poorly. The friend in Shanghai is Japanese. Not only can he speak Chinese, but he can also write Chinese characters.

A: What language do you speak with them?

啊		a	part.	ah
会	會	huì	aux.	can; be able to
说	說	shuō	v.	to speak
话	話	huà	n.	(spoken) language

第六课 我的两个朋友

（A——丁一，B——张三）

A：你有中国朋友吗？

B：我没有中国朋友，可是，我有两个在中国的朋友。

A：他们在哪儿啊？

B：一个在北京，一个在上海。

A：他们会不会说中国话？

B：在北京的朋友是美国人，会说一点儿中文，可是说得不好。在上海的朋友是日本人，他不但会说中国话，而且会写中国字。

A：你跟他们说什么话？

中国话	中國話	Zhōngguó huà	n.	the Chinese language
一点儿	一點兒	yìdiǎnr	num.	a little bit
写	寫	xiě	v.	to write
跟		gēn	prep.	with

B: Wǒde Měiguó péngyou xǐhuān gēn wǒ shuō Yīngwén, kěshì wǒde Yīngwén bùhǎo, chángcháng tīngbudǒng tā shuōdehuà. Wǒ juéde tā shuō Yīngwén shuōde tàikuàile. Wǒ qǐng tā shuōde màn yìdiǎnr. Yàoshì tā mànmānr de shuō, wǒ jiù tīngdedǒng le.

A: Nǐ gēn Rìběn péngyou shuō shénme huà?

B: Wǒ zhǐhuì shuō Zhōngwén, búhuì shuō Rìwén, suǒyǐ wǒ gēn tā shuō Zhōngwén.

A: Tāde Zhōngwén shuōde hǎobùhǎo?

B: Tāde Zhōngwén shuōde hěnhǎo, kěshì yǒu jǐge zì, tā zǒngshì shuō de bútàihǎo, xiàng Rìběn de "rì," hé rèchá de "rè."

A: Rìběn rén huì xiě Zhōngguó zì, suǒyǐ Rìběn rén juéde xiě Zhōngguó zì hěn róngyì, kěshì Měiguó rén juéde hěnnán.

B: My American friend likes to speak English with me, but my English is not very good. I frequently cannot understand what he says. I think he speaks English too fast. I ask him to speak a little slower. If he speaks slowly, then I can understand him.

A: What language do you speak with your Japanese friend?

B: I can only speak Chinese. I cannot speak Japanese, so I talk with him in Chinese.

A: Does he speak Chinese well?

B: He speaks Chinese very well, but there are a few words that he always says not very well, like the "rì" in "Rìběn" and the "rè" in "rèchá."

A: Japanese people can write Chinese characters. Therefore, Japanese people think that writing Chinese characters is very easy, but American people think that it is very hard.

常常		chángcháng	adv.	often
听	聽	tīng	v.	to listen
懂		dǒng	v./adj.	to understand; understood
觉得	覺得	juéde	v.	to feel, to think
快		kuài	adj.	fast, quick

B：我的美国朋友喜欢跟我说英文，可是我的英文不好，常常听不懂他说的话。我觉得他说英文说得太快了，我请他说得慢一点儿。要是他慢慢儿地说，我就听得懂了。

A：你跟日本朋友说什么话？

B：我只会说中文，不会说日文，所以我跟他说中文。

A：他的中文说得好不好？

B：他的中文说得很好，可是有几个字，他总是说得不太好，像日本的"日"和热茶的"热"。

A：日本人会写中国字，所以日本人觉得写中国字很容易，可是美国人觉得很难。

请	請	qǐng	v.	to politely ask (somebody to do …)
慢		màn	adj.	slow
要是……就……		yàoshì … jiù…	conj.	if … then …
地		de	part.	adverbial phrase modifier marker
慢慢儿地V.P.		mànmānr de	adv.	to slowly do something
几	幾	jǐ	num.	several
总是	總是	zǒngshì	adv.	always
像		xiàng	prep.	such as …
热	熱	rè	adj.	hot (in temperature)
容易		róngyì	adj.	easy

语法 Grammar Notes

1. Complex Modifier

A modifier of a noun or a noun phrase can be a simple noun (e.g., 中国朋友), an adjective (e.g., 好朋友), or a pronoun (e.g., 我的朋友). It can also have a more complex form in which it is itself a phrase or even a clause. In that case, the particle 的 is added between the modifier phrase or clause and what is being modified. In this text, we see examples of propositional phrases used as noun modifiers:

▶ 在中国的朋友
  zài Zhōngguó de péngyou
  friends who are in China

The modifier can be expanded by adding more elements:

在中国的美国朋友
zài Zhōngguó de Měiguó péngyou
American friends who are in China

Besides prepositional phrases, other forms of phrases can be used as noun modifiers as well:

Verb phrase as modifier: 喜欢说中文的美国朋友
Xǐhuān shuō Zhōngwén de Měiguó péngyou
American friends who like to speak Chinese

Adjective phrase as modifier: 很聪明的美国朋友
Hěn cōngming de Měiguó péngyou
American friends who are very smart

Note:

a. The modifier always precedes the central noun in Chinese, no matter how long the modifier is or how many elements it contains.

b. When translated between Chinese and English, the complex noun modifier in Chinese usually corresponds to the English relative clause started by which, that, who, whom, and so on.

c. Although in theory a modifier can be extended unlimitedly by adding different elements, Chinese people tend not to use very long modifiers. It is better to break a lengthy modifier into short sentences.

d. When translating such phrases from Chinese into English, always begin your translation with the noun or noun phrase that follows 的.

2. 啊

Particle 啊 has different connotations when used in different contexts. It can be used independently or as an end-of-word or end-of-sentence particle. Its functions include expressing emotions such as a strong opinion, enthusiasm, or mild reproach, softening a question, and summoning one's attention. In this lesson, 啊 is at the end of a question to soften the tone, making it sound less abrupt. With or without 啊, the meaning of the question does not change at all.

▶ 他们在哪儿啊？
Tāmen zài nǎr a?
Where are they?

你是不是学生啊？
Nǐ shìbúshì xuéshēng a?
Are you a student?

Note: If there is already the question particle 吗 or 呢 at the end of the sentence, 啊 cannot be added.

3. 一个……，一个…… (one … one …)

This sentence structure is used to describe two or three things (usually no more than three) in a parallel situation. Measure word 个 can be replaced by other more appropriate measure words according to the context.

▶ 一个在北京，一个在上海。
Yíge zài Běijīng, yíge zài Shànghǎi.
One (friend) is in Beijing; one (friend) is in Shanghai.

我有两本书，一本是中文书，一本是英文书。
Wǒ yǒu liǎngběn shū, yìběn shì Zhōngwén shū, yìběn shì Yīngwén shū.
I have two books, one is a Chinese book, and one is an English book.

4. Auxiliary Verb 会 (can, be able to do)

An auxiliary verb (also called a helping verb) is a verb that gives further semantic or syntactic information about the main verb following it. Verbs such as can, may, must, will, and shall are all a special kind of auxiliary verb called the modal verb.

会, often translated into English as "can," actually has a narrower range of meaning in Chinese. It emphasizes the ability or skill of doing something that is acquired through learning, that is, "can" in the sense of "know how to."

Positive form: Subject + 会 + V.P.
Negative form: 不会 + V.P.
Question form: 会不会 + V.P.

▶ 他们会不会说中国话？
Tāmen huìbúhuì shuō Zhōngguóhuà?
Can they speak Chinese?

▶ 他不但会说中国话，而且会写中国字。
Tā búdàn huì shuō Zhōngguó huà, érqiě huì xiě Zhōngguó zì.
He not only can speak Chinese, but also can write Chinese characters.

5. 说 (to speak, to say)

When the verb 说 is not followed by an object, such as a language or a direct quotation, or by a complement such as 说得很好, it needs to take the dummy object 话. For example, to translate "She likes to talk" into Chinese, one would say 他喜欢说话 instead of 他喜欢说, which sounds incomplete.

6. 一点儿 (a little bit)

There are two major usages of 一点儿, both of which appear in this lesson.

(1) 一点儿 + noun   a little bit of something

一点儿 can be used as a noun modifier, which means it can modify only nouns or noun phrases. 一点儿 CANNOT be used to modify adjectives or verbs, as when one translates sentences such as "I am a little bit hungry" or "I kind of like him/like him a little bit." A different phrase that fits these situations will be introduced later.

▶ 在北京的朋友会说一点儿中文。
Zài Běijīng de péngyou huì shuō yìdiǎnr Zhōngwén.
The friend in Beijing can speak a little Chinese.

我想喝一点儿咖啡。
Wǒ xiǎng hē yìdiǎnr kāfēi.
I want to drink a little coffee.

(2) As an adjective complement

Adj. + 一点儿

In this case, 一点儿 has the connotation of comparison: a little bit more … (compared to the previous situation mentioned in context). This sense of comparison can be implicit without the use of 比 (to compare) in the sentence; but it can also be explicit:

A 比 B adj. 一点儿	A is a little bit more adj. than B

Compare this to what we learned in Lesson 5:

A 比 B adj. 得多	A is much more adj. than B

▶ 慢一点儿
màn yìdiǎnr
a little bit slower

我妹妹比你高一点儿。
Wǒ mèimei bǐ nǐ gāo yìdiǎnr.
My younger sister is a little bit taller than you.

7. Verb Complements

In Chinese, elements (usually verbs and adjectives) that follow a main verb to provide additional information about the action are called verb complements. Verb complements describe the status or development of the action, and they usually come after the main verb. Verb complements can be divided into three major categories.

(1) Descriptive complement

The first category to be introduced here is the descriptive complement. Complements that describe the style of an action are called descriptive complements, such as "He speaks **well**" or "He runs **fast**." Use the following structures for descriptive complements:

Positive: (verb + object +) verb + 得 + modifier + complement
Negative: (verb + object +) verb + 得 + 不 + complement
Question: (verb + object +) verb 得 complement 不 complement

▶ 他说英文说得太快了。
Tā shuō Yīngwén shuō de tàikuàile.
He speaks English too fast.

▶ 他会说一点儿中文，可是说得不好。
Tā huìshuō yìdiǎnr Zhōngwén, kěshì shuōde bùhǎo.
He can speak a little Chinese, but he doesn't speak well.

他说英文说得快不快？

Tā shuō Yīngwén shuō de kuàibúkuài?

Does he speak English fast?

Note:

a. 得 is the complement marker that is placed between the main verb and the complement.

b. When there is an object, one needs to repeat the verb.

c. Note that 的 and 得 are pronounced in exactly the same way but are written differently and have very different grammatical functions.

(2) Potential complement

The second category of verb complements is the potential complement. Potential complements describe whether the attempt to perform the action of the verb can attain the result expressed by the complements, such as "I **can** understand" or "He **cannot** run **fast**." Use the following structures to form potential complements:

Positive: verb + 得 + complement (+ object)
Negative: verb + 不 + complement (+ object)
Question: verb 得 complement + verb 不 complement (+ object)

我听得懂他说的话。

Wǒ tīngdedǒng tā shuōdehuà.

I can understand what he said.

我听不懂他说的话。

Wǒ tīngbudǒng tā shuōdehuà.

I cannot understand what he said.

他说的话，你听得懂听不懂？

Tā shuōdehuà, nǐ tīngdedǒng tīngbudǒng?

Can you understand what he said?

In the above examples of potential verb complements, the object of each sentence, that is, 他说的话 (what he said), can be put either after the verb + complement or at the beginning of the sentence, as seen in the last example. This is a major difference between the descriptive and the potential verb complements.

(3) Resultative complements

Complements that describe the result, effect, or extent of an action are called resultative complements, such as "He **finished eating** dinner." These will be further discussed in future lessons.

The descriptive verb complements that are introduced in this lesson are listed in the following table for your reference:

DESCRIPTIVE VERB COMPLEMENTS	
Positive	**Negative**
好 (说中文) 说得很好 Speak (Chinese) well (写中国字) 写得很好 Write Chinese characters well	(说中文) 说得不好 Speak (Chinese) poorly (写中国字) 写得不好 Write Chinese characters poorly
快 说得太快了 Speak too fast	说得不快 Speak not fast
慢 写得很慢 Write very slowly 写得慢一点儿 Write a little slower	写得不慢 Write not slowly

8. Topic-Comment Sentences

"Topic-comment" is a very common structure in Chinese. The topic serves as a substantive, but it does not have to be a noun or noun phrase. It can also be an adjective, a verb, a full predicate, or a whole sentence. In meaning, the relation between topic and comment is also quite flexible, rather like the English "As for [topic], say [comment]."

▶ 他的中文说得好不好？
Tāde Zhōngwén shuōde hǎobuhǎo?
Does he speak Chinese well? (literally: As for his Chinese, does he speak well?)

In this example in the text, "他的中文" (his Chinese) is the topic, and "speak well or not" is the comment. In such a pattern, the topic is moved to the front position and thus is emphasized. The sentence can be reorganized in the regular order without changing the meaning.

他说中文说得好不好？
Tā shuō Zhōngwén shuōde hǎobuhǎo?.

Study the following examples:

Topic	Comment
说中国话 Shuō Zhōngguó huà	不难 bùnán.

Literal translation: As for speaking Chinese, it's not difficult.
Natural translation: It is not difficult to speak Chinese.

Topic	Comment
你写的书 Nǐ xiě de shū	我不喜欢 Wǒ bù xǐhuān.

Literal translation: As for the book you wrote, I don't like.
Natural translation: I don't like the book you wrote.

9. 跟 Somebody V.P. (do something with somebody)

In most cases, prepositional phrases (such as 跟 somebody) precede the main verb in Chinese, just opposite to the case in English. When one negates the sentence, the negative marker 不 or 没有 needs to be put in front of the preposition.

Positive form: 我的朋友跟我说英文。
Wǒde péngyou gēn wǒ shuō Yīngwén.
My friend speaks English with me.

Negative form: 我的朋友不跟我说英文。
Wǒde péngyou bù gēn wǒ shuō Yīngwén.
My friend doesn't speak English with me.

Positive form: 我跟我的妹妹喝咖啡。
Wǒ gēn wǒde mèimei hē kāfēi.
I have coffee with my younger sister.

Negative form: 我不跟我的妹妹喝咖啡。
Wǒ bùgēn wǒde mèimei hē kāfēi.
I don't have coffee with my younger sister.

10. 慢慢儿地说 (to speak slowly)

An adverbial phrase used as a modifier in front of the verb describes the manner in which the action is carried out. 慢 is pronounced "màn" by itself; however, Chinese people customarily pronounce the second 慢 in the first tone in the phrase 慢慢儿地 (mànmānr de). In addition to 慢慢儿地 说, one can say 慢慢儿地写 (write slowly), 慢慢儿地吃 (eat slowly), and so on, indicating a slow and patient manner without rushing.

Note: Usually 快 is NOT used in the same way to denote a fast pace.

Compared with the descriptive verb complement, verb 得很慢 (do something very slowly), the adverbial phrase 慢慢儿地＋verb emphasizes the manner of the action and it is often used in an imperative sentence. Verb 得很慢 describes the actual performance of the action and carries with it a slightly unsatisfactory tone.

The other common adverbial phrase with a repetitive form is 好好儿地 (do something in a good and diligent manner). Similarly, the second 好 is pronounced in the first tone in the phrase 好好儿地 (hǎohāor de). For example: 好好儿地学中文 (study Chinese hard).

11. 觉得 (to think, to feel (about something based on experience))

觉得 is a frequently used word to express one's opinion and is often translated as "to think" or "to feel."

Subject + 觉得 + clause

The clause after 觉得 can be a statement or a question. To negate the sentence, negate the clause after 觉得.

▶ 我觉得他说英文说得太快了。
　　Wǒ juéde tā shuō Yīngwén shuōde tàikuàile .
　　I think he speaks English too fast.

你觉得他会不会说中文？
　　Nǐ juéde tā huìbúhuì shuō Zhōngwén?
　　Do you think if he can speak Chinese?

我觉得他不会说中文。
　　Wǒ juéde tā búhuì shuō Zhōngwén.
　　I think he cannot speak Chinese.

12. 要是……就…… (if ... then ...)

要是 subject 1 V.P.1, subject 2 就 V.P.2

Note:

a. The two subjects in the two clauses can be the same or different.

b. In many cases, 要是 can be dropped out, and one will decide whether it is an "if" sentence according to the context.

▶ 要是他慢慢儿地说，我就听得懂了。
　　Yàoshì tā mànmānr de shuō, wǒ jiù tīngdedǒng le.
　　If he speaks slowly, I will be able to understand.

要是你妹妹没有男朋友，我就请她喝咖啡。
　　Yàoshì nǐ mèimei méiyǒu nán péngyou, wǒ jiù qǐng tā hē kāfēi.
　　If your younger sister doesn't have a boyfriend, I will invite her to coffee.

13. 了

In Lesson 5, we discussed 了 used to indicate action completed. In this lesson 了 is to indicate the appearance of a new situation or a change of situation.

> ▶ 要是他慢慢儿地说，我就听得懂了。
> Yàoshì tā mànmānr de shuō, wǒ jiù tīngdedǒng le.
> If he speaks slowly, I will be able to understand.

In the above example, the speaker could not understand his friend's English because he speaks too fast. If the friend speaks slowly, then a new situation in which the speaker is able to understand his friend will appear. This new situation is signified by the use of 了 at the end of the sentence.

> 我有男朋友了。
> Wǒ yǒu nán péngyou le.
> I have a boyfriend (now).

(了 indicates the change of situation from not having a boyfriend in the past to having a boyfriend now)

> 我会说中文了。
> Wǒ huìshuō Zhōngwén le.
> I can speak Chinese (now).

(了 indicates that the speaker changes from unable to speak Chinese to now being able to speak it)

14. Adverbs

只　　only, just
总是　always

All Chinese adverbs precede the main verb or adjective in the sentence.

> ▶ 我只会说中文。
> Wǒ zhǐ huì shuō Zhōngwén.
> I can only speak Chinese.

> 桌子上只有一本书。
> Zhuōzi shang zhǐ yǒu yìběnshū.
> There is only one book on the table.

> ▶ 他总是说得不太好。
> Tā zǒngshì shuō de bútàihǎo.
> He always doesn't say it very well.

他总是跟我说英文。

Tā zǒngshì gēn wǒ shuō Yīngwén.

He always speaks English with me.

15. To Identify a Character

To identify a letter to avoid confusion or mistake in English, one will choose a frequently used word as a reference. For example, "a" as in "apple." Chinese has a similar way to identify a character by relating it to a common word.

▶ 热茶的"热"

rèchá de "rè"

"rè" as in the word "rèchá"

中国的"中"

Zhōngguó de "zhōng"

"zhōng" as in the word "Zhōngguó"

16. 像A, B, C (such as A, B, C)

像 is used to introduce a list of items as examples to support a previous statement.

▶ 有几个字，他总是说得不太好，像日本的"日"和热茶的"热"。

Yǒu jǐge zì, tā zǒngshì shuō de bútàihǎo, xiàng Rìběn de "rì" hé rèchá de "rè."

There are a few words that he always says not very well: such as the "rì" in "Rìběn" and the "rè" in "rè chá."

桌子上有很多东西，像书、纸，和笔。

Zhuōzi shang yǒu hěnduō dōngxi, xiàng shū, zhǐ, hé bǐ.

There are many things on the table, such as books, paper, and pens.

Traditional Character Text

我的兩個朋友

（A——丁一，B——張三）

A：你有中國朋友嗎？

B：我沒有中國朋友，可是，我有兩個在中國的朋友。

A：他們在哪兒啊？

B：一個在北京，一個在上海。

A：他們會不會說中國話？

B：在北京的朋友是美國人，會說一點兒中文，可是說得不好。在上海的朋友是日本人，他不但會說中國話，而且會寫中國字。

A：你跟他們說什麼話？

B：我的美國朋友喜歡跟我說英文，可是我的英文不好，常常聽不懂他說的話。我覺得他說英文說得太快了，我請他說得慢一點兒。要是他慢慢兒地說，我就聽得懂了。

A：你跟日本朋友說什麼話？

B：我只會說中文，不會說日文，所以我跟他說中文。

A：他的中文說得好不好？

B：他的中文說得很好，可是有幾個字，他總是說得不太好，像日本的"日"和熱茶的"熱"。

A：日本人會寫中國字，所以日本人覺得寫中國字很容易，可是美國人覺得很難。

7 Xuǎnkè
(Choosing Classes)

Pinyin Text

(A—Lǐ Sì, B—Zhāng Sān de māma, C—Zhāng Sān)

A: Wéi, qǐngwèn Zhāng Sān zài ma?

B: Zhāng Sān búzài. Qǐngwèn nín shì něiwèi a?

A: Wǒ shì tāde tóngxué Lǐ Sì. Nín yǒu Zhāng Sān de shǒujī hàomǎ ma?

B: Zhāng Sān de shǒujī hàomǎ shì èrlíngbāsìyīyīqī.

A: Shénme? shì sìqīqīqī ma? Qǐngnín zàishuō yícì.

B: Búshì sìqīqīqī, shì sìyāoyāoqī

A: Xièxie.

B: Búkèqi.

****

English Translation

(A—Li Si, B—Zhang San's mother, C—Zhang San)

A: Hello. May I ask if Zhang San is there?

B: Zhang San is not here. May I ask who's calling?

A: This is his classmate, Li Si. Do you have Zhang San's cell phone number?

B: Zhang San's cell phone number is 208-4117.

A: What? Is it 4777? Please say it one more time.

B: It is not 4777. It is 4117.

A: Thank you.

B: You are welcome.

****

选	選	xuǎn	v.	to choose, to pick, to select
喂		wéi	inter.	hello
问	問	wèn	v.	to ask
请问	請問	qǐngwèn	phrase	May I ask …
在		zài	v.	to be here/there
位		wèi	m.w.	honorific measure word for people
哪位		něiwèi		which one (person), who

第七课 选课

（A——李四，B——张三的妈妈，C——张三）

A：喂，请问张三在吗？

B：张三不在。请问您是哪位啊？

A：我是他的同学李四。您有张三的手机号码吗？

B：张三的手机号码是208-4117。

A：什么？是4777吗？请您再说一次。

B：不是4777，是4117 (sì-yāo-yāo-qī)。

A：谢谢。

B：不客气。

****

同学	同學	tóngxué	n.	classmate
李		Lǐ	n.	Li, a common Chinese surname
手机	手機	shǒujī	n.	cell phone
号码	號碼	hàomǎ yāo	n. num.	(phone, room, etc.) number "1" a variation for one, pronounced "yāo" when used in phone number or room number
再		zài	adv.	again, one more time

A: Wéi, shì Zhāng Sān ma?

C: Shì, wǒ shì Zhāng Sān, qǐngwèn nín shì něiwèi?

A: Wǒshì Lǐ Sì. Wǒ zuótiān gěi nǐ dǎ diànhuà, kěshì nǐ búzài. Zhèige xuéqī nǐ mángbumáng?

C: Lǐ Sì a, wǒ tàimángle. Zhèige xuéqī wǒ xuǎnle yìmén Zhōngwén kè, cóng xīngqī yī dào xīngqī wǔ měitiān dōu děi shàngkè. Chúle shàngkè yǐwài, háiyǒu kǎoshì, tīngxiě, tīng lùyīn, xiě Zhōngguó zì. Měitiān dōu yǒu zuòbuwán de zuòyè.

A: Nǐ hǎoxiàng bútài xǐhuān Zhōngwén kè.

A: Hello, is this Zhang San?

C: Yes, this is Zhang San. May I ask who's speaking?

A: This is Li Si. I called you yesterday, but you were not there. Are you busy this semester?

C: Li Si, I'm too busy. This semester I chose a Chinese class, and we have to go to class every day from Monday to Friday. Besides going to class, we also have to take tests and dictations, listen to recordings, and write Chinese characters. Every day I have homework that I can't finish.

A: It seems that you don't like Chinese class very much.

昨天		zuótiān	t.w.	yesterday
给	給	gěi	prep.	to, for (somebody)
电话	電話	diànhuà	n.	telephone; phone call
打电话	打電話	dǎ diànhuà	v.o.	to make a phone call
学期	學期	xuéqī	n.	semester
门	門	mén	m.w.	for classes (on various subjects)
从A到B	從A到B	cóng … dào…	prep.	from … to …
星期一		xīngqī yī	n.	Monday
星期五		xīngqī wǔ	n.	Friday

A：喂，是张三吗？

C：是，我是张三，请问您是哪位？

A：我是李四。我昨天给你打电话，可是你不在。这个学期你忙不忙？

C：李四啊，我太忙了。这个学期我选了一门中文课，从星期一到星期五每天都得上课。除了上课以外，还有考试、听写、听录音、写中国字。每天都有做不完的作业。

A：你好像不太喜欢中文课。

每天		měitiān	t.w.	every day
得		děi	aux. v.	have to …
上课	上课	shàngkè	v.o.	to attend class
除了……以外		chúle … yǐwài	conj.	besides, except for
还	還	hái	adv.	in addition, furthermore
考试	考試	kǎoshì	n.	test, examination
听写	聽寫	tīngxiě	n.	dictation quiz
录音	錄音	lùyīn	n.	recording
做		zuò	v.	to do
完		wán	adj.	finished
做不完		zuòbuwán	v.c.	cannot finish
作业	作業	zuòyè	n.	homework, assignment
好像		hǎoxiàng	adv.	It seems that …

C: Búshì, búshì, wǒ hěn xǐhuān Zhōngwén kè. Zhōngwén kè máng shì máng, kěshì fēicháng yǒu yìsi. Nǐ zhèige xuéqī xuǎnle shénme kè a?

A: Wǒ xuǎnle yìmén Yīngwén, yìmén lìshǐ, yìmén yīnyuè, háiyǒu yìmén shùxué.

C: Zhèixiē kè nǐ dōu xǐhuān ma?

A: Wǒ zuì xǐhuān yīnyuè kè, zuì bù xǐhuān shùxué kè. Shùxué kè de lǎoshī shì ge Zhōngguó rén, tā shuō Yīngwén shuōde bùhǎo, wǒ chángcháng tīngbudǒng tā shuō de huà.

C: No, no, I like Chinese class very much. Yes, Chinese class is busy, but it is extremely interesting. What classes did you choose this semester?

A: I chose an English class, a history class, a music class, and a math class.

C: Do you like all these classes?

A: My favorite is music class, and my least favorite is math class. My math teacher is Chinese, and he does not speak English well. I often cannot understand what he says.

C：不是，不是，我很喜欢中文课。中文课忙是忙，可是非常有意思。你这个学期选了什么课啊？

A：我选了一门英文，一门历史，一门音乐，还有一门数学。

C：这些课你都喜欢吗？

A：我最喜欢音乐课，最不喜欢数学课。数学课的老师是个中国人，他说英文说得不好，我常常听不懂他说的话。

非常		fēicháng	adv.	extremely
有意思		yǒu yìsi	adj.	interesting
历史	歷史	lìshǐ	n.	history
音乐	音樂	yīnyuè	n.	music
数学	數學	shùxué	n.	math
这些	這些	zhèixiē	pron.	these

语法 Grammar Notes

1. 请问 (May I ask ...)

To express politeness when asking for information, one often begins the question with the phrase 请问. It is similar to "May I ask ..." or "Excuse me ..." in English.

▶ 请问，张三在吗？

Qǐngwèn, Zhāng Sān zài ma?

Excuse me, is Zhang San there?

请问，您会写中国字吗？

Qǐngwèn, nín huì xiě Zhōngguózì ma?

May I ask if you know how to write Chinese characters?

喂 is used at the beginning of a phone conversation. If you initiate the phone call and know the other party, you can say: 喂，请问，是X吗？(Hello, is this X?). If you are the receiver of a phone call and do not know who is calling, you can ask "喂，请问，您哪位" (Hello, may I ask who is calling).

2. The Honorific Measure Word 位

The measure word for a person is 个. But 位 is a preferable alternative if you want to show respect for the person addressed or referred to. 位 cannot be followed directly by 人 without a modifier, so it is wrong to say 一位人, but it is correct to say 一位老人 (an old man). 位 can be combined with determinatives 这，那，哪 to serve as the subject or object.

▶ 请问您是哪位？

Qǐngwèn nínshì něiwèi?

May I ask who you are?

我们的数学老师是一位好老师。

Wǒmén de shùxué lǎoshī shì yíwèi hǎo lǎoshī.

Our math teacher is a good teacher.

3. Subject 在/不在

In the sentence "请问，张三在吗？" 在 is used as the main verb. If both parties know the place talked about, the place word after 在 can be omitted, and 在/不在 can be used independently as a predicate to indicate whether someone is at some place or not.

4. 给 Somebody 打电话 (to call somebody)

Preposition 给 here means "to, toward," indicating the direction of the action.

▶ 我昨天给你打电话，你不在。
Wǒ zuótiān gěi nǐ dǎdiànhuà, nǐ búzài.
I called you yesterday, but you weren't there.

他每天都给妈妈打电话。
Tā měitiān dōu gěi māma dǎ diànhuà.
He calls his mother every day.

5. 除了……以外

除了……以外 can appear in two different constructions, and thus can have two different meanings depending on which construction is used. 以外 is optional.

a. 除了A以外，……也/还……

This is the "inclusive use" of 除了, which can be translated into "in addition to. …" This pattern shows that, even after the inclusion of A, the general truth still holds.

▶ 除了上课以外，还有考试、听写。
Chúle shàngkè yǐwài, háiyǒu kǎoshì, tīngxiě.
In addition to going to classes, there are also examinations and dictations.

除了音乐课，我觉得数学课也很有意思。
Chúle yīnyuè kè, wǒ juéde shùxuékè yě hěn yǒu yìsi.
In addition to music class, I also think math class is very interesting.

b. 除了A以外，……都……

This is the "exclusive use" of 除了, which can be translated into "except" or "with the exception of. …" This pattern shows an explicit exclusion of A before making a statement.

▶ 除了张三以外，我的朋友都去过北京。
Chúle Zhāng Sān yǐwài, wǒde péngyou dōu qùguo Běijīng.
Except Zhang San, all my (other) friends have been to Beijing.

除了写中国字以外，我觉得学中文不难。
Chúle xiě Zhōngguó zì yǐwài, wǒ juéde xué Zhōngwén bùnán.
Except writing Chinese characters, I find studying Chinese not difficult.

6. 从A到B (from A to B)

This pattern is used to show the distance/scope between two points A and B. A and B can either both be place words or time words.

▶ 从星期一到星期五每天都得上课。

Cóng xīngqīyī dào xīngqīwǔ měitiān dōu děi shàngkè.

We have to go to class every day from Monday to Friday.

我们每天从9点到10点都有中文课。

Wǒmen měitiān cóng jiǔdiǎn dào shídiǎn dōu yǒu zhōngwénkè.

We have Chinese class from 9 to 10 every day.

7. Auxiliary verb 得 (have to do ...)

Subject 得 + V.P.

我得去纽约工作。

Wǒ děi qù Niǔyuē gōngzuò.

I have to go to New York to work.

There is not a direct negative form of 得. To express the meaning of "don't have to" or "not necessary to do something," one usually uses búyòng 不用, which will be introduced later.

8. Review: The Completive 了

了 serves a variety of functions and may appear either after a verb or at the end of a sentence. In this text, 了 appeared as a completive 了 after a verb. This verb-了 indicates completion of an action. See also grammar note 8 in Lesson 5.

interrogative form: **V. 了(O.) 吗? or V. 了(O.) 没有?**

affirmative form: **Subject V. 了(O.)**

negative form: **没(有) V. O.**

Note: The negative form does NOT include 了.

▶ 你这个学期选了什么课啊？

Nǐ zhèige xuéqī xuǎnle shénme kè a?

What classes did you choose this semester?

我选了一门英文，一门数学。我没选历史。

Wǒ xuǎnle yìmén Yīngwén, yìmén shùxué. Wǒ méixuǎn lìshǐ.

I chose English and math. I didn't choose history.

Since a past action is generally also a completed action, the verb- 了 is often used in such a temporal context. However, the concept of completion of an action is different from the concept of a past action. For many English speakers, the idea of "completed action" mistakenly seems synonymous with the past tense. An example of how the completive 了 can be used for an action taking place in the present or future is:

我明天做完了作业给你打电话。

Wǒ míngtiān zuòwán le zuòyè gěi nǐ dǎ diànhuà.

I will call you (after) I finish doing my homework tomorrow.

If the completive aspect is not stressed in the context, the verb- 了 is not used even when the verb refers to a past action. When the sentence describes a habitual action in the past, 了 should not be used. Also, when 说, 问 appear in the sentence, if the emphasis is on the content of the speech, 了 should not be used. For example, 昨天他说请我喝咖啡 (Yesterday he said that he would invite me to coffee).

9. 完 (finished, complete) as a Verb Complement

We have learned the following verbs that often take 完 as complement: 做，吃，写，听. The potential positive and negative forms are given below.

做得完 able to finish doing   做不完 unable to finish doing
吃得完 able to finish eating   吃不完 unable to finish eating
写得完 able to finish writing   写不完 unable to finish writing
听得完 able to finish listening   听不完 unable to finish listening

10. 好像 (It seems that ...)

好像 is inserted before a sentence or a predicate to mean "it seems that. ..."

▶ 你好像不太喜欢中文课。

Nǐ hǎoxiàng bútài xǐhuān zhōngwén kè.

It seems that you don't like Chinese class very much.

好像他也选了音乐课。

Hǎoxiàng tā yě xuǎnle yīnyuè kè.

It seems that he also chose music class.

11. Verb/adj. 是 verb/adj., 可是……

This is a colloquial expression to indicate concession. It means "yes, the given statement is true, but. …"

▶ 中文课忙是忙，可是非常有意思。

Zhōngwén kè máng shì máng, kěshì fēicháng yǒu yìsi.

Yes, Chinese class is busy, but it's very interesting.

北京烤鸭油是油，可是我很喜欢吃。

Běijīng kǎoyā yóushìyóu, kěshì wǒ hěn xǐhuān chī.

Although Beijing roast duck is oily, I like to eat it very much.

12. The Indefinite Measure Word 些

The indefinite measure word for nouns is 些. It is used before plural nouns of unspecified reference. The most commonly used combinations of determinative + indefinite measure word are 这些 (these), 那些 (those), 哪些 (which), 一些 (some), and 有些 (some).

▶ 这些课你都喜欢吗？

Zhèixiē kè nǐ dōu xǐhuān ma?

Do you like all these classes?

有些课我喜欢，有些课我不喜欢。

Yǒuxiē kè wǒ xǐhuān, yǒuxiē kè wǒ bù xǐhuān.

Some classes I like, some I don't like.

Traditional Character Text

選課

（A——李四，B——張三的媽媽，C——張三）

A：喂，請問張三在嗎？

B：張三不在。請問您是哪位啊？

A：我是他的同學李四。您有張三的手機號碼嗎？

B：張三的手機號碼是208-4117。

A: 什麼？是4777嗎？請您再説一次。

B: 不是4777，是4117。

A：謝謝。

B：不客氣。

****

A：喂，是張三嗎？

C：是，我是張三，請問您是哪位？

A：我是李四，我昨天給你打電話，可是你不在。這個學期你忙不忙？

C：李四啊，我太忙了。這個學期我選了一門中文課，從星期一到星期五每天都得上課。除了上課以外，還有考試，聽寫，聽錄音，寫中國字。每天都有做不完的作業。

A：你好像不太喜歡中文課。

C：不是，不是，我很喜歡中文課。中文課忙是忙，可是非常有意思。你這個學期選了什麼課啊？

A：我選了一門英文，一門歷史，一門音樂，還有一門數學。

C：這些課你都喜歡嗎？

A：我最喜歡音樂課，最不喜歡數學課。數學課的老師是個中國人，他說英文說得不好，我常常聽不懂他說的話。

Kàn bu Qīngchǔ
(Cannot See Clearly)

Pinyin Text

(A—Dīng Yī, B—lǎoshī)

A: Lǎoshī, hēibǎn shang de zì tàixiǎole, wǒ kàn bu qīngchǔ, qǐng nín bǎ zì xiě de dà yìdiǎnr.

B: Hēibǎn shang de zì bìngbuxiǎo a, nǐ shì kàn bu qīngchǔ, háishì kànbudǒng?

A: Yǒude zì wǒ kàn bu qīngchǔ, yǒude zì wǒ kànbudǒng.

B: Něige zì nǐ kàn bu qīngchǔ, něige zì nǐ kànbudǒng?

A: Dìwǔ ge zì wǒ kàn bu qīngchǔ, dìsān ge zì wǒ kànbudǒng.

English Translation

(A—Ding Yi, B—teacher)

A: Teacher, the writing on the blackboard is too small. I can't see it clearly. Would you please write the characters a little larger?

B: The characters on the blackboard are actually not small. Is it that you can't see them clearly or that you can't understand them?

A: There are some characters that I can't see clearly and some that I can't understand.

B: Which characters can you not see clearly, and which can you not understand?

A: I can't see the fifth character clearly, and I can't understand the third character.

看	kàn	v.	to look, to watch
清楚	qīngchǔ	adj./adv.	clear; clearly
黑板	hēibǎn	n.	blackboard

第八课 看不清楚

（A——丁一，B——老师）

A：老师，黑板上的字太小了，我看不清楚，请您把字写得大一点儿。

B：黑板上的字并不小啊，你是看不清楚，还是看不懂？

A：有的字我看不清楚，有的字我看不懂。

B：哪个字你看不清楚，哪个字你看不懂？

A：第五个字我看不清楚，第三个字我看不懂。

把		bǎ	part.	pre-object marker
并	並	bìng	adv.	actually (not)
有的		yǒude	pron.	some

B: Hǎo, wǒ bǎ dìwǔ ge zì xiě de dà yìdiǎnr, xiànzài nǐ kàn qīngchǔ le ma?

A: Háishì kàn bu qīngchǔ.

B: Dìwǔ ge zì xiěde yòu dà yòu qīngchǔ, kěshì nǐ háishì kàn bu qīngchǔ, nǐ děi zuò dào qiánbiānr lái.
(xuéshēng zuòdào le dìyīpái)
Xiànzài nǐ kàn qīngchǔ le ma?

A: Kàn shì kàn qīngchǔ le, kěshì, wǒ bùdǒng zhèige zì de yìsi.

B: Xiǎo Dīng, nǐ búdàn yǎnjīng yǒu wèntí, érqiě nǎozi yěyǒu wèntí. Zhèige zì shì "Xiǎo Dīng" de "dīng" zì a!

A: Shì "dīng" zì a! Gāngcái wǒ méi kàn qīngchǔ, wǒ yǐwéi shì "shàngxià" de "xià" zì.

B: Okay, I will write the fifth character larger. Now do you see it clearly?

A: I still can't see it clearly.

B: The fifth character is written both large and clearly, but you still can't see it clearly. You have to come sit in the front.
(The student moves to the first row)
Now do you see it clearly?

A: I can see it clearly, all right, but I don't understand that character's meaning.

B: Xiao Ding, not only do your eyes have problems, but your brain also has problems! This character is the "dīng" as in "Xiǎo Dīng!"

A: Oh, it's "dīng!" Just now I didn't see it clearly. I thought it was the "xià" as in "shàngxià."

还是	還是	háishì	adv.	still
又……又……		yòu … yòu …	conj.	both … and …
坐		zuò	v.	to sit
到		dào	prep.	destination marker "to some place"
前边(儿)	前邊(兒)	qiánbiān(r)	n.	front
来	來	lái	directional complement	
排		pái	m.w.	row

B：好，我把第五个字写得大一点儿，现在你看清楚了吗？

A：还是看不清楚。

B：第五个字写得又大又清楚，可是你还是看不清楚，你得坐到前边儿来。（学生坐到了第一排）现在你看清楚了吗？

A：看是看清楚了，可是，我不懂这个字的意思。

B：小丁，你不但眼睛有问题，而且脑子也有问题。这个字是"小丁"的"丁"字啊！

A：是"丁"字啊! 刚才我没看清楚，我以为是"上下"的"下"字。

意思		yìsi	n.	meaning
眼睛		yǎnjīng	n.	eye
问题	問題	wèntí	n.	problem, question
脑子	腦子	nǎozi	n.	mind; brain
刚才	剛才	gāngcái	t.w.	just now
以为	以爲	yǐwéi	v.	to think (incorrectly about something)
上下		shàngxià	n.	up and down, on and below

语法 Grammar Notes

1. Resultative Verb Complements

In Lesson 6 we talked about descriptive verb complements and potential verb complements. The verb complements in this lesson that fall into these two categories are listed in the following table:

DESCRIPTIVE COMPLEMENTS		POTENTIAL COMPLEMENTS	
Positive	Negative	Positive	Negative
写得大一点儿 write a little bigger		看得清楚 can see clearly	看不清楚 cannot see clearly
		看得懂 can understand by seeing	看不懂 cannot understand by seeing

The third category of verb complements that is to be discussed in this lesson is the resultative verb complement, which describes the result, effect, or extent of an action. Use the following pattern to form resultative verb complements:

> Positive: verb + complement + 了
> Negative: 没(有) + verb + complement
> Question: verb + complement + 了 + 没有

For example:

看清楚了	kàn qīngchǔ le	saw clearly
没看清楚	méi kàn qīngchǔ	did not see clearly
看懂了	kàndǒng le	understood by seeing
没看懂	méi kàndǒng	did not understand by seeing

2. 把 Structure

> Subject + 把 + object + v. + $\begin{cases} \text{resultative complement} \\ \text{other elements} \end{cases}$

When an object and a resultative verb complement appear in the same sentence, Chinese people try not to put both elements after the verb to avoid confusion. In such cases, pretransive 把 is used to move the object before the verb, therefore solving the problem. The best way to master the usage of

把 is to memorize and imitate examples; however, to facilitate your understanding of the structure, here are some rules and tips:

(1) When to use the 把 structure？

When the subject causes changes in the object through some action, one may use the 把 structure. The change of the object is reflected in the elements after the verb, and there are two possible situations:

a. The action changes the status of the object: the element after the verb is a resultative complement. Both examples from this lesson fall into this category:

▶ 请您把字写得大一点儿。
Qǐng nín bǎ zì xiě de dàyìdiǎnr.
Please write the characters a little larger.

▶ 我把第五个字写得大一点儿。
Wǒ bǎ dìwǔge zì xiě de dà yìdiǎnr.
I will write the fifth character a little larger.

Note:
*** The smallest possible resultative complement is 了.
*** There are a few exceptions where certain resultative complements cannot be used in the 把 structure. These will be discussed later.

b. The action changes the location of the object. This situation will be explained later. An example would be: "I put the book on the table" ("on the table" is the new location of the object "book" caused by the action "to put").

(2) In the 把 structure, the object has to be a definite object and cannot be indefinite. For example, the object can be "**the** character" but not "**a** character," can be "**the** cup of coffee" or "**the** book" but cannot be any cup of coffee or book.

3. 并不/并没有 (actually not)

This structure is used to negate or argue against the previous positive statement or assumption about the topic.

▶ 黑板上的字并不小啊。
Hēibǎn shang de zì bìngbuxiǎo a.
The characters on the blackboard are actually not small.

我并没有哥哥。
Wǒ bìng méiyǒu gēge.
I actually do not have an older brother.

4. 有的(+ noun)……有的(+ noun)…… (some … some …)

有的……有的…… is a parallel structure that describes different portions of a large group. The noun after 有的 can be dropped out when it is understood in context. Grammatically, 有的…… 有的…… is identical to 一个……一个…… (one … one … ; see Lesson 6). The only difference is that 有的 mostly refers to plural nouns, while 一个 always refers to singular nouns.

▶ 有的字我看不清楚，有的字我看不懂。
　　Yǒude zì wǒ kàn bu qīngchǔ, yǒude zì wǒ kànbudǒng.
　　There are some characters that I can't see clearly and some that I can't understand.

我有很多朋友，有的是美国人，有的是日本人。
Wǒ yǒu hěnduō péngyou, yǒude shì Měiguó rén, yǒude shì Rìběn rén.
I have many friends; some are Americans and some are Japanese.

5. 还是 (adv.) (still)

还是 is interchangeable with 还 to mean "still." When the verb is 是, use 还 instead of 还是 to avoid the repetition of 是.

▶ 我还是看不清楚。
　　Wǒ háishì kàn bu qīngchǔ.
　　I still cannot see clearly.

The other function of 还是 is to connect the two alternatives in a selective question.

　　是A 还是B 　 Is it A or B?

The example from this lesson reads,

▶ 你是看不清楚，还是看不懂？
　　Nǐ shì kànbu qīngchǔ, háishì kànbudǒng?
　　Is it that you can't see them clearly or that you can't understand them?

6. 又……又…… (both … and …)

又……又…… is a parallel structure that describes two corresponding characteristics or actions of the subject. The elements after 又 must either both be adjectives or both be verb phrases. They have to be both positive or both negative, and not contradictory or unrelated.

▶ 第五个字写得又大又清楚。
　　Dìwǔge zì xiěde yòu dà yòu qīngchǔ.
　　The fifth character is written both large and clearly.

那个美国学生又会说中文，又会说日文。

Nèige Měiguó xuéshēng yòuhuì shuō Zhōngwén, yòuhuì shuō Rìwén.

That American student can speak both Chinese and Japanese.

7. Destination Marker 到

到 signifies the new location of the subject or object. When the location of the object changes, use the 把 structure. In this lesson, we will discuss only the situation in which the location of the subject changes.

Subject + v. + 到 + place word (destination)

▶ 你得坐到前边儿来。

Nǐ děi zuòdào qiánbiānr lái.

You have to come sit in the front (of the room).

8. Simple Directional Complement 来

In the sentence 你得坐到前边儿来 (You have to come sit in the front), 来, which originally is a verb "to come," indicates that the direction of the subject's action is toward the speaker. In this scenario, the speaker is the teacher who is in the front of the classroom and the subject is the student. The student moves toward the teacher and sits in the front of the room. 来 is transformed from an action verb to a directional complement. There are two basic directional complements:

来：The movement is toward the speaker
去：The movement is away from the speaker

Verb + direction + 来/去

你坐到前边儿去.

Nǐ zuòdào qiánbiānr qù.

You go and sit in the front.

(The speaker is in the back of the room, and the subject moves away from the speaker to sit in the front of the room.)

9. Review 不但……而且/也……

For an explanation of the sentence pattern 不但……而且……, see Lesson 5. The adverb 也 can be inserted into the second clause as an emphatic element, but it does not change the meaning of the sentence at all. One may use both 而且 and 也 in the second clause or use just one of them.

When the subjects for the two clauses are the same:

Subject 不但 V.P.1, 而且也 V.P.2

When the subjects are different:

Subject 1 不但 V.P., 而且 subject 2 也 V.P.

▶ 你不但眼睛有问题，脑子也有问题。

Nǐ búdàn yǎnjīng yǒu wèntí, nǎozi yěyǒu wèntí.

Not only do your eyes have problems, but your brain also has problems.

不但数学课的作业很多，中文课的作业也很多。

Búdàn shùxuékè de zuòyè hěnduō, Zhōngwénkè de zuòyè yě hěnduō.

Not only math class has a lot of homework, but Chinese class also has a lot of homework.

10.　有问题

有问题 has two interpretations, that is, "to have a question" and "to have a problem." One has to choose the correct meaning according to the context.

老师，我有问题。

Lǎoshī, wǒ yǒu wèntí.

Teacher, I have questions.

他的眼睛有问题，看不清楚黑板上的字。

Tāde yǎnjīng yǒu wèntí, kàn bu qīngchǔ hēibǎn shang de zì.

His eyes have problems; he can't see the characters on the blackboard clearly.

11. 以为 (to think incorrectly about something)

Subject 以为 + clause

以为 and 觉得 are both used to express one's opinion; however, 以为 indicates that the speaker's original opinion was different from the fact.

▶ 刚才我没看清楚，我以为是"上下"的"下"字。

Gāngcái wǒ méi kàn qīngchǔ, wǒ yǐwéi shì "shàngxià" de "xià" zì.

Just now I didn't see it clearly. I thought it was the "xià" as in "shàngxià."

那个日本人说中文说得很好，我以为他是中国人。

Nèige Rìběn rén shuō Zhōngwén shuōde hěnhǎo, wǒ yǐwéi tā shì Zhōngguó rén.

That Japanese person speaks Chinese very well. I thought he was Chinese.

Traditional Character Text

看不清楚

（A——丁一，B——老師）

A：老師，黑板上的字太小了，我看不清楚，請您把字寫得大一點兒。

B：黑板上的字並不小啊。你是看不清楚，還是看不懂？

A：有的字我看不清楚，有的字我看不懂。

B：哪個字你看不清楚，哪個字你看不懂？

A：第五個字我看不清楚，第三個字我看不懂。

B：好，我把第五個字寫得大一點兒，現在你看清楚了嗎？

A：還是看不清楚。

B：第五個字寫得又大又清楚，可是你還是看不清楚，你得坐到前邊來。（學生坐到了第一排）現在你看清楚了嗎？

A：看是看清楚了，可是，我不懂這個字的意思。

B：小丁，你不但眼睛有問題，腦子也有問題。這個字是"小丁"的"丁"字啊。

A：是"丁"字啊！剛才我沒看清楚，我以為是"上下"的"下"字。

Hēchá Háishì Hēkāfēi
(To Drink Tea or Coffee)

Pinyin Text

(A—Zhāng Sān, B—Dīng Yī)

A: Nǐ hēchá háishì hē kāfēi?

B: Chá hé kāfēi wǒ dōu bùhē, wǒ hē bīngshuǐ.

A: Zhèijiā fànguǎnr de kāfēi hěnhǎo, nǐ wèishénme bùhē ne?

B: Wǎnshàng hē kāfēi wǒ shuìbuzháo, suǒyǐ wǎnshàng wǒ bùhē kāfēi.

A: Nǐ shénme shíhou hē kāfēi?

B: Wǒ měitiān zǎoshàng dōu hē liǎngbēi kāfēi. Zǎoshàng bùhē kāfēi, wǒ xǐng bú guòlái.

A: Zhōngguó rén dàduō hēchá, hěnshǎo hē kāfēi, yě hěnshǎo chī tiándiǎn.

English Translation

(A—Zhang San, B—Ding Yi)

A: Will you drink tea or coffee?

B: I will drink neither tea nor coffee. I will drink ice water.

A: This restaurant's coffee is very good, why don't you drink it?

B: If I drink coffee at night, I can't sleep. Therefore I don't drink coffee at night.

A: When do you drink coffee?

B: I drink two cups of coffee every morning. If I don't drink coffee in the morning, I can't wake up.

A: Chinese people mostly drink tea. They rarely drink coffee, and they also rarely eat dessert.

冰		bīng	n.	ice
水		shuǐ	n.	water
家	傢	jiā	m.w.	measure word for restaurants, stores, companies, etc.
饭馆(儿)	飯館(兒)	fànguǎn(r)	n.	restaurant
晚上		wǎnshàng	n.	evening, night

第九课 喝茶还是喝咖啡

（A——张三，B——丁一）

A：你喝茶还是喝咖啡？

B：茶和咖啡我都不喝，我喝冰水。

A：这家饭馆儿的咖啡很好，你为什么不喝呢？

B：晚上喝咖啡，我睡不着，所以晚上我不喝咖啡。

A：你什么时候喝咖啡？

B：我每天早上都喝两杯咖啡。早上不喝咖啡，我醒不过来。

A：中国人大多喝茶，很少喝咖啡，也很少吃甜点。

睡		shuì	v.	to sleep
睡不着		shuìbuzháo	v.c.	cannot fall asleep
什么时候		shénme shíhou	q.w.	when, what time
早上		zǎoshàng	t.w.	morning
杯		bēi	m.w	a cup of
醒		xǐng	v.	to wake
醒不过来	醒不過來	xǐngbúguòlái	v.c.	cannot wake up
大多		dàduō	adv.	mostly
少		shǎo	adj.	little, few
甜点	甜點	tiándiǎn	n.	dessert

B: Měiguó rén chīle wǎnfàn yǐhòu, xǐhuān chī tiándiǎn, xiàng bīngqílín hé dàngāo dōu shì wǒ zuì xǐhuān de.

A: Zhōngguó rén chīle wǎnfàn yǐhòu, chángcháng chī yìdiǎnr shuǐguǒ, xiàng xīguā, xiāngjiāo hé júzi dōushì wǒ chángchī de.

B: Měiguó rén hé Zhōngguó rén chīfàn de xíguàn yǒudiǎnr bùtóng.

A: Shì a, Zhōngguó rén yòng kuàizi chīfàn, Měiguó rén yòng dāochā chīfàn.

B: Měiguó rén xiān hētāng, zài chīfàn. Zhōngguó rén xiān chīfàn, zài hētāng.

B: After having dinner, Americans like to eat dessert, like ice cream and cake. Those are my favorites.

A: After having dinner, Chinese people often eat a little bit of fruit, like watermelon, bananas, and tangerines. Those are all fruits I frequently eat.

B: Americans' and Chinese people's eating habits are a little different.

A: Yes, Chinese use chopsticks while Americans use a knife and fork to eat.

B: Americans have soup first, and then eat their meal. Chinese people eat their meal first, and then have soup.

饭	飯	fàn	n.	meal
晚饭	晚飯	wǎnfàn	n.	dinner
以后	以後	yǐhòu	prep.	after
冰淇淋		bīngqílín	n.	ice cream
蛋糕		dàngāo	n.	cake
水果		shuǐguǒ	n.	fruit
西瓜		xīguā	n.	watermelon
香蕉		xiāngjiāo	n.	banana
桔子		júzi	n.	tangerine
习惯	習慣	xíguàn	n.	habit

B：美国人吃了晚饭以后，喜欢吃甜点，像冰淇淋和蛋糕都是我最喜欢的。

A：中国人吃了晚饭以后，常常吃一点儿水果，像西瓜、香蕉和桔子都是我常吃的。

B：美国人和中国人吃饭的习惯有点儿不同。

A：是啊，中国人用筷子吃饭，美国人用刀叉吃饭。

B：美国人先喝汤，再吃饭；中国人先吃饭，再喝汤。

有(一)点儿點	yǒu(yì)diǎnr	adv.	a little
不同	bùtóng	n./adj.	difference; different
用	yòng	v.	to use
筷子	kuàizi	n.	chopsticks
刀叉	dāochā	n.	knife and fork
先	xiān	adv.	first
汤　　　湯	tāng	n.	soup
再	zài	adv.	then

A: Jīntiān de wǎnfàn zhēnhǎo, yòu yǒu yú, yòu yǒu ròu. Xièxie nǐ qǐngwǒ chīfàn.

B: Jīntiān búdàn chī de hěnhǎo, yě tán de hěn gāoxìng.

A: Zhèicì nǐ qǐng wǒ chīfàn, xiàcì wǒ qǐng nǐ hē kāfēi.

A: Today's dinner was really good. There was both fish and meat. Thank you for inviting me to dinner.

B: Not only did we eat well today, we also had a very nice conversation.

A: This time you took me out to eat. Next time I will take you out for coffee.

A：今天的晚饭真好，又有鱼，又有肉。谢谢你请我吃饭。

B：今天不但吃得很好，也谈得很高兴。

A：这次你请我吃饭，下次我请你喝咖啡。

鱼	鱼	yú	n.	fish
肉		ròu	n.	meat
谈	談	tán	v.	to talk
高兴	高興	gāoxìng	adj.	happy
这次	這次	zhèicì	n.	this time
下次		xiàcì	n.	next time

语法 Grammar Notes

1. A, B … , Subject 都 V. P.

To translate a sentence with "both/all" (都) or with "neither/none" (都不/都没有), it is better to put the objects at the beginning of the sentence.

▶ 茶和咖啡我都不喝。
Chá hé kāfēi wǒ dōu bùhē.
I drink neither tea nor coffee.

历史课和音乐课我都选了。
Lìshǐkè hé yīnyuékè wǒ dōu xuǎn le.
I took both the history class and the music class.

2. Particle 呢

In Lesson 5, we saw the particle 呢 following a phrase to form a follow-up question or a question understood, that is, 妈妈呢？(How about mother?) In this lesson, 呢 is used at the end of a question to soften the tone, making the question sound not so abrupt.

▶ 你为什么不喝呢？
Nǐ wèishénme bùhē ne?
Why don't you drink it?

他有几个中国朋友呢？
Tā yǒu jǐge Zhōngguó péngyou ne?
How many Chinese friends does he have?

Note: When another particle such as 吗 or 啊 is already at the end of the sentence, one cannot add 呢 to it.

3. Measure Words

In addition to the general measure word 个, we have seen several special measure words that are used for specific nouns in the previous lessons:

一本书	a book	一张纸/照片	a piece of paper/photo
一位老师	a teacher	一门课	a course

Two new measure words introduced in this lesson are:

家 (used for stores, restaurants, etc.)：这家饭馆　　this restaurant

杯：一杯咖啡　　a cup of coffee

Note: The special feature that is noteworthy of measure words such as 家 and 杯 is that they themselves are nouns and must be modified by other measure words when used as nouns and combined with numbers or determinatives such as 几, 这, 那, and 每. For example:

家 (originally means "home, family")：　一个家　　a home/a family

杯子 (originally means "cup," and it has to take the suffix 子 to function as a noun)：

一个杯子　　a cup.

Measure word for action: 次　　time, instance

Different from measure words for nouns that precede the modified noun, 次, which describes the number of times that an action occurs, is inserted between the verb it modifies and the object of the verb (if it is available).

吃一次饭　　chī yícì fàn　　have a meal once

喝两次咖啡　　hē liǎngcì kāfēi　　have coffee twice

Two other common phrases with 次：

这 (一) 次　　this time　　　　下 (一) 次　　next time

4. Verb Complements: 着, 过来, 高兴

着 (pronounced "zháo") and 过来, when used as verb complements, have special meanings and are combined with specific verbs. Please memorize the combination as a whole unit.

	Descriptive complements	Potential complements		Resultative complements	
		Positive	Negative	Positive	Negative
着	N/A	睡得着 can fall asleep	睡不着 cannot fall asleep	睡着了 fell asleep	没睡着 did not fall asleep
过来	N/A	醒得过来 can wake up	醒不过来 cannot wake up	醒过来了 woke up	没醒过来 did not wake up

高兴 (happy) is a frequently used adjective itself. When used as a verb complement, it usually appears in the descriptive form.

▶ 今天不但吃得很好，也谈得很高兴。

Jīntiān búdàn chīde hěnhǎo, yě tán de hěn gāoxìng.

Not only did we eat well today, but we also had a very nice conversation.

他听音乐听得很高兴。

Tā tīng yīnyuè tīngde hěn gāoxìng.

He enjoyed listening to the music (literally: He listened to the music happily).

5. Subject 大多 VP1，很少 VP2 (mostly … rarely …)

▶ 中国人大多喝茶，很少喝咖啡，也很少吃甜点。

Zhōngguórén dàduō hēchá, hěnshǎo hē kāfēi, yě hěnshǎo chī tiándiǎn.

Chinese people usually drink tea. They rarely drink coffee, and they also rarely eat dessert.

我的中国朋友大多跟我说英文，很少说中文。

Wǒde Zhōngguó péngyou dàduō gēn wǒ shuō Yīngwén, hěnshǎo shuō Zhōngwén.

My Chinese friends mostly speak English with me, and they rarely speak Chinese (with me).

6. A 跟 B (有一点儿) 不同 (A is (a little different) from B)

▶ 美国人跟中国人吃饭的习惯有点儿不同。

Měiguó rén gēn Zhōngguó rén chīfàn de xíguàn yǒudiǎnr bùtóng.

Americans' and Chinese people's eating habits are a little different.

中国茶跟日本茶有点儿不同。

Zhōngguó chá gēn Rìběn chá yǒudiǎnr bùtóng.

Chinese tea is a little bit different from Japanese tea.

Note: (1) In this sentence pattern, 跟 is interchangeable with 和.
        (2) 一 can be dropped out and one can just say 有点儿.

7. 用 Something V.P.

用, originally a verb "to use," can be used to introduce the tools or manner with which the action is performed. When negating the sentence, one needs to put 不 in front of 用, the first position verb.

▶ 中国人用筷子吃饭，美国人用刀叉吃饭。

Zhōngguó rén yòng kuàizi chīfàn, Měiguó rén yòng dāochā chīfàn.

Chinese people use chopsticks while Americans use a knife and fork to eat.

中国人不用刀叉吃饭。

Zhōngguó rén búyòng dāochā chīfàn.

Chinese people do not use a knife and fork to eat.

8. Action Series: 先 V.P.1 再 V.P.2 (first ... then ...)

先 and 再 are both adverbs used to narrate a series of consecutive actions.

▶ 美国人先喝汤，再吃饭；中国人先吃饭，再喝汤。

Měiguó rén xiān hētāng, zài chīfàn. Zhōngguó rén xiān chīfàn, zài hētāng.

Americans have soup first and then eat their meal. Chinese people eat their meal first and then have soup.

我们先上中文课，再上数学课。

Wǒmen xiān shàng Zhōngwén kè, zài shàng shùxué kè.

We have Chinese class first and then math class.

9. Pivotal Sentence

The sentence "我请你喝咖啡" can be divided into two short sentences:

我请你。 (I invite you.) 你喝咖啡。 (You drink coffee)

The object of the first sentence 你 is also the subject of the second sentence. 你 functions as a pivot to combine two kernel sentences into one longer sentence, which is called a pivotal sentence. In a pivotal structure, the first kernel sentence must be a subject-verb-object sentence, while the second one may have a variety of forms. The following sentence is another example of pivotal structure:

老师请我坐到前边儿去。

Lǎoshī qǐng wǒ zuòdào qiánbiānr qù.

The teacher asked me to sit in the front.

The two kernel sentences are:

老师请我。   我坐到前边儿去。

我 is the pivot here.

Cultural Notes

Starbucks in China

In the early 1990s, drinking coffee was still an unusual and sometimes even exotic habit in China. The stereotypical impression of coffee for common Chinese people was that it looked and tasted like traditional Chinese medicine, which was very unpleasant. Such experiences were mostly obtained from early instant coffee products. Except for a few coffee shops in international hotels in big cities, there was no easy way for Chinese people to try coffee.

Along with the rapid economic growth in the late 1990s, all kinds of Western products and services were introduced to China and became popular among Chinese customers. Coffee is one of them. Today, coffee is just one of the numerous beverages that people can choose from, and it is especially popular among young people and professionals.

The American coffee shop chain Starbucks arrived in China in 1999 and launched its first shop in Beijing. Now, they have opened more than eight hundred stores in more than fifty cities in Mainland China. Its Chinese name is 星巴克 (xīngbākè). "Xīng" means star in Chinese and "bākè" is used only to imitate the sound of "bucks." If you visit Beijing, Shanghai, or any of the major cities in China, you will find young Chinese baristas working at Starbucks in familiar green aprons; you can order from an almost identical menu, and pay about the same price as you do in the United States. Several years ago, Starbucks even operated a store in Beijing's Forbidden City, which used to be the imperial palace and has now been converted into a national museum. This attracted much media attention and aroused heated discussion among Chinese people: is it a symbol of globalization or a sign of Western erosion of traditional Chinese culture?

Traditional Character Text

喝茶還是喝咖啡

（A——張三，B——丁一）

A：你喝茶還是喝咖啡？

B：茶和咖啡我都不喝，我喝冰水。

A：這家飯館兒的咖啡很好，你爲什麽不喝呢？

B：晚上喝咖啡，我睡不着，所以晚上我不喝咖啡。

A：你什麽時候喝咖啡？

B：我每天早上都喝兩杯咖啡。早上不喝咖啡，我醒不過來。

A：中國人大多喝茶，很少喝咖啡，也很少吃甜點。

B：美國人吃了晚飯以後，喜歡吃甜點，像冰淇淋和蛋糕都是我最喜歡的。

A：中國人吃了晚飯以後，常常吃一點兒水果，像西瓜、香蕉和桔子都是我常吃的。

B：美國人和中國人吃飯的習慣有點兒不同。

A：是啊，中國人用筷子吃飯，美國人用刀叉吃飯。

B：美國人先喝湯，再吃飯；中國人先吃飯，再喝湯。

A：今天的晚飯真好，又有魚，又有肉。謝謝你請我吃飯。

B：今天不但吃得很好，也談得很高興。

A：這次你請我吃飯，下次我請你喝咖啡。

10

Dàizhe Yǎnjìngr Zhǎo Yǎnjìngr (Looking for Glasses While Wearing Them)

Pinyin Text

(A— Dīng Yī, B— Zhāng Sān)

A: Wǒde "yǎnjing" bújiànle, nǐ kàndào le ma?

B: Yǎnjing búshì zhǎng zài tóushang ma? Zěnme bújiànle ne? Nǐ shuōde shì "yǎnjìngr" ba.

A: Duì, duì, wǒ zhǎo wǒde yǎnjìngr, búshì yǎnjing. Wǒ de yǎnjìng bùhǎo, méiyǒu yǎnjìngr, shénme dōu kàn bu qīngchǔ.

B: Wǒ gāngcái kàndào nǐde yǎnjìngr zài zhuōzi shang. Nǐ kànkan zàibúzài nàr.

A: Wǒ kàn le, bú zài nàr.

B: Zàibúzài diànnǎo shàngbiānr?

A: Diànnǎo shàngbiānr yě méiyǒu.

English Translation

(A— Ding Yi, B— Zhang San)

A: I don't see my eyes. Do you see them?

B: Aren't your eyes on your head? How can you not know where they are? Don't you mean your "glasses?"

A: Yes, yes, I am looking for my glasses, not my eyes. My eyes are not very good. If I'm not wearing my glasses, I can't see anything clearly.

B: I just saw your glasses on the desk. Take a look and see if they are there.

A: I looked. They are not there.

B: Are they on top of the computer?

A: They are not on the computer, either.

戴		dài	v.	to wear (cap, glove, accessories)
着		zhe	v. suffix	
眼镜(儿)	眼鏡(兒)	yǎnjìng(r)	n.	eyeglasses
找		zhǎo	v.	to look for
不见了	不見了	bújiànle	phrase	… is missing
看到		kàndào	v.c.	to see

第十课 戴着眼镜儿找眼镜儿

（A——丁一，B——张三）

A：我的"眼睛"不见了，你看到了吗？

B：眼睛不是长在头上吗？怎么不见了呢？你说的是"眼镜儿"吧？

A：对，对，我找我的眼镜儿，不是眼睛。我的眼睛不好，没有眼镜儿，什么都看不清楚。

B：我刚才看到你的眼镜儿在桌子上，你看看在不在那儿。

A：我看了，不在那儿。

B：在不在电脑上边儿？

A：电脑上边儿也没有。

长	長	zhǎng	v.	to grow
头		tóu	n.	head
怎么	怎麼	zěnme	q.w.	how come
对	對	duì	adj.	correct, right
那儿		nàr	p.w.	there, over there
电脑	電腦	diànnǎo	n.	computer

B: Zàibúzài diànnǎo hé dǎyìnjī de zhōngjiān?

A: Wǒ yě kàn le. Diànnǎo hé dǎyìnjī de zhōngjiān yě méiyǒu yǎnjìngr.

B: Chōuti lǐbiānr nǐ zhǎo le ma?

A: Zhǎo le, nǎr dōu zhǎo le, háishi zhǎobuzháo.

B: Chuáng xiàbiānr yě kàn le ma?

A: Kàn—le—, chuáng xiàbiānr yě méiyǒu wǒde yǎnjìngr.

B: Nándào nǐde yǎnjìngr zhǎngle tuǐ, zìjǐ pǎo chūqu le ma? Nǐ qù wūzi wàibiānr zhǎozhao.

A: Bù kěnéng. Wǒ jīntiān gēnběn méi chūqu.

B: Wǒ kàndào le, kàndào le. Yǎnjìngr jiùzài nǐ tóushang ne. Nǐ dàizhe yǎnjìngr zhǎo yǎnjìngr, zěnme zhǎodezháo a?

B: What about between the computer and the printer?

A: I also looked there, but my glasses are not between the computer and the printer.

B: Did you look inside the drawer?

A: I checked there. I have checked everywhere, but I still can't find them.

B: Did you also look under the bed?

A: I ALREADY LOOKED. My glasses are not under the bed either.

B: Did your glasses grow legs and walk away on their own? Look for them outside of the room.

A: That is impossible. Today I haven't gone out at all.

B: I see them; I see them! Your glasses are on top of your head. You were looking for your glasses while you were wearing them. How could you find them?

打印机	打印機	dǎyìnjī	n.	printer
抽屉	抽屜	chōuti	n.	drawer
里边(儿)	裡邊(兒)	lǐbiānr	prep.	inside of…
找不着		zhǎobuzháo	v.c.	cannot find
床	牀	chuáng	n.	bed
难道	難道	nándào	adv.	Doesn't the subject … ?
腿		tuǐ	n.	leg

B：在不在电脑和打印机的中间？

A：我也看了，电脑和打印机的中间也没有眼镜儿。

B：抽屉里边儿你找了吗？

A：找了，哪儿都找了，还是找不着。

B：床下边儿也看了吗？

A：看——了——，床下边儿也没有我的眼镜儿。

B：难道你的眼镜儿长了腿，自己跑出去了吗？你去屋子外边儿找找。

A：不可能，我今天根本没出去。

B：我看到了，看到了，眼镜儿就在你头上呢。你戴着眼镜儿找眼镜儿，怎么找得着啊？

自己		zìjǐ	pron.	oneself
跑		pǎo	v.	to run
出去		chūqu	v.c.	to go out
屋子		wūzi	n.	room; house
外边(儿)	外邊(兒)	wàibiānr	prep.	outside of
可能		kěnéng	adj./adv.	possible; possibly
根本		gēnběn	adv.	(not) at all
就		jiù	adv.	simply, just
找得着		zhǎodezháo	v.c.	can find

语法 Grammar Notes

1. 着

着 has two functions and two pronunciations.

(1) As a verb suffix it is pronounced as *zhe*.

It is added after a status verb to indicate a continuing state.

▶ 戴着眼镜儿找眼镜儿
Dàizhe yǎnjìngr zhǎo yǎnjìngr
Looking for glasses while wearing them

他坐着看书。
Tā zuòzhe kànshū.
He is/was sitting (there) reading.

(2) As a verb complement it is pronounced as *zháo*. It is also added after a verb to indicate the result of attainment or successful completion. 找 and 睡 are two most common verbs that can take 着 as complement.

▶ potential complement:
找得着／找不着 zhǎodezháo/zhǎobuzháo   can/cannot find
睡得着／睡不着 shuìdezháo/shuìbuzháo   can/cannot fall asleep

resultative complement:
找着了／没找着 zhǎozháole/méizhǎozháo   found/did not find
睡着了／没睡着 shuìzháole/méishuìzháo   fell/did not fall asleep

2. 到 as a Verb Complement

Similar to 着, 到 can be used as a verb complement to indicate attainment of an action. Verbs that are often combined with 到 include 找，看，听.

看 to look　　　　看到 to see
听 to listen　　　听到 to hear
找 to look for　　找到 to find

▶ 我刚才看到你的眼镜儿在桌子上。
Wǒ gāngcái kàndào nǐde yǎnjìngr zài zhuōzi shang.
I just saw your glasses on the desk.

他找到了他的眼镜儿。
Tā zhǎodào le tāde yǎnjìngr.
He found his glasses.

3. Rhetorical Questions

There are three forms of rhetorical questions in this lesson.

(1) Subject 不是 V.P. 吗?　　　Isn't it true that … ?
(2) Subject 怎么 V.P. 呢?　　　How come … /how … ?
(3) 难道 + subject + V.P. (吗)?Does the subject not … ? (In this pattern, the subject is movable. It can be placed before or after 难道.)

▶ 眼睛不是长在头上吗？怎么不见了呢？
Yǎnjing búshì zhǎngzài tóushang ma? Zěnme bújiàn le ne?
Aren't your eyes on your head? How can you not know where they are?

他不是中国人吗？怎么不会说中文呢？
Tā búshì Zhōngguó rén ma? Zěnme búhuì shuō Zhōngwén ne?
Isn't he Chinese? How come he can't speak Chinese?

难道你不喜欢吃北京烤鸭吗？
Nándào nǐ bù xǐhuān chī Běijīng kǎoyā ma?
Don't you like to eat Beijing roast duck?

Note: 会 appears in the first two examples above, which represent the two meanings of 会 as an auxiliary verb. In both cases, 会 is translated as "can" in English; however, in the first example "怎么会不见了呢？" 会 indicates a future possibility, while in the second example "不会说中文," 会 refers to one's ability to do something through acquisition.

4. Question Pronoun 都 V.P.

The question pronouns that are often used in this pattern include 什么 (what), 哪儿 (where), 谁 (who), and 哪 (which). When the question word is used in a statement with 都, it simply means "all" or "none" in the sense of being all-inclusive or all-exclusive. The position of the subject is movable. The subject can be put between the question pronoun and the adverb 都. If used in a context where the subject is understood, like the example below from this lesson, the subject can be omitted.

▶ 没有眼镜儿，什么都看不清楚。

Méiyǒu yǎnjìngr, shénme dōu kàn bu qīngchǔ.

Without glasses, [I] cannot see anything clearly.

This example is a conditional sentence. 没有 + noun phrase, "If without something or somebody, the subject will. ..." In this pattern, the word "if" is sometimes dropped, but the meaning is still implied.

哪儿都是你的书。

Nǎr dōushì nǐde shū.

Your books are everywhere.

5. Statement + 吧

In Lesson 4, we discussed the function of 吧 at the end of a statement to form a suggestion. It can be translated as "let's" or "how about." For example:

我们去吃饭吧。

Wǒmen qù chīfàn ba.

Let's go eat.

In this lesson, 吧 is used to transform a statement into speculation, similar to the English "I suppose," indicating that the speaker believes that the statement is true, but is not quite sure.

▶ 你说的是眼镜儿吧？

Nǐ shuōde shì yǎnjìngr ba?

You must be talking about your eyeglasses.

你是学生吧？

Nǐ shì xuéshēng ba?

You must be a student.

6. Review: Location

A 在B的上边/下边/里边/外边/左边/右边/旁边

(alternative forms: 上头/下头/里头/外头)

A is on top of/under/inside of/outside of/left of/right of/beside B

A 在B和C的中间

A is between B and C

7. 可能/不可能 (adj./adv.) (possible (possibly)/impossible (impossibly))

可能 and 不可能 can be used as simple answers to various questions.

When used as adverbs, they follow the rule of position for all adverbs and should be put between the subject and the verb.

那个中国人可能不会说英文。

Nèige Zhōngguó rén kěnéng búhuì shuō Yīngwén.

That Chinese probably cannot speak English.

你的书可能在桌子上。

Nǐde shū kěnéng zài zhuōzi shang.

Your book is possibly on the desk.

8. 根本不/没(有) + V.P. (not at all)

The adverb 根本 has to be followed by a negative phrase: 不 for habitual action and 没(有) for action not completed.

▶ 我今天根本没出去。

Wǒ jīntiān gēnběn méi chūqu.

I haven't gone out at all today.

我根本没看到你的眼镜儿。

Wǒ gēnběn méi kàndào nǐde yǎnjìngr.

I didn't see your glasses at all.

你根本不是我的朋友。

Nǐ gēnběn búshì wǒde péngyou.

You are not my friend at all.

9. Pronoun + 自己 (oneself)

Personal pronouns and nouns, singular or plural, can combine with 自己. For example, 我自己 (myself). 自己 can also be used by itself as a pronoun or modifier.

▶ 难道你的眼镜儿长了腿，自己跑出去了吗？

Nándào nǐde yǎnjìngr zhǎngle tuǐ, zìjǐ pǎo chūqu le ma?

Did your eyeglasses grow legs and walk away on their own?

自己的事，自己做。

Zìjǐ de shì, zìjǐ zuò.

One does one's matter on one's own.

10. 就 + Verb

就 here means "merely, simply," or "just" to emphasize the immediate or common place nature of the action.

▶ 眼镜儿就在你头上呢。

Yǎnjìngr jiùzài nǐ tóushang ne.

Your eyeglasses are right on top of your head.

Traditional Character Text

戴著眼鏡兒找眼鏡兒

（A——丁一，B——张三）

A：我的"眼睛"不見了，你看到了嗎？

B：眼睛不是長在頭上嗎？怎麼不見了呢？你説的是"眼鏡兒"吧？

A：對，對，我找我的眼鏡兒，不是眼睛。我的眼睛不好，沒有眼鏡兒，什麼都看不清楚。

B：我剛才看到你的眼鏡兒在桌子上，你看看在不在那兒。

A：我看了，不在那兒。

B：在不在電腦上邊兒？

A：電腦上邊兒也沒有。

B：在不在電腦和打印機的中間？

A：我也看了，電腦和打印機的中間也沒有眼鏡兒。

B：抽屜裏邊兒你找了嗎？

A：找了，哪兒都找了，還是找不着。

B：床下邊兒也看了嗎？

A：看——了——，床下邊兒也沒有我的眼鏡兒。

B：難道你的眼鏡兒長了腿，自己跑出去了嗎？你去屋子外邊兒找找。

A：不可能，我今天根本沒出去。

B：我看到了，看到了，眼鏡兒就在你頭上呢。你戴著眼鏡兒找眼鏡兒，怎麼找得着啊？

Shéi Chī le Wǒ de Dōngxi?
(Who Ate My Stuff?)

Pinyin Text

(A—Zhāng Sān, B—Lǐ Sì, C—Dīng Yī)

A: Wǒ fàngzài bīngxiāng lǐ de sānpíng kělè hé liǎngbāo bǐnggān zěnme dōu bú jiàn le ne?

B: Wǒ méichī nǐde dōngxi.

A: Kěndìng shì Xiǎo Dīng chī de.

B: Shàngge xīngqī tā bǎ wǒde píngguǒ, júzi, xiāngjiāo, hé hànbǎobāo dōu chīdiào le.

A: Xiǎo Dīng bǎ nǐde zhōngfàn chīdiào le, nà nǐchī shénme ne?

English Translation

(A—Zhang San, B—Li Si, C—Ding Yi)

A: How come the three bottles of cola and two bags of cookies that I put in the refrigerator are all gone?

B: I didn't eat your stuff.

A: It must be Xiaoding who ate them.

B: Last week he ate up all my apples, oranges, bananas, and hamburgers.

A: Xiao Ding ate up your lunch; then what did you eat?

放		fàng	v.	to put something at some place
冰箱		bīngxiāng	n.	refrigerator
瓶		píng	n./m.w.	bottle; a bottle of
可乐	可樂	kělè	n.	cola
包		bāo	n./m.w.	bag; a bag of

第十一课 谁吃了我的东西

（A——张三，B——李四，C——丁一）

A：我放在冰箱里的三瓶可乐和两包饼干怎么都不见了呢？

B：我没吃你的东西。

A：肯定是小丁吃的。

B：上个星期他把我的苹果、桔子、香蕉和汉堡包都吃掉了。

A：小丁把你的中饭吃掉了，那你吃什么呢？

肯定		kěndìng	adv.	most probably, must be
苹果	蘋果	píngguǒ	n.	apple
上个(星期)		shàngge	adj.	last (week)
中饭	中飯	zhōngfàn	n.	lunch
掉		diào	v.c.	finished; done
那		nà	pron.	in that case, then

B: Bīngxiāng lǐ háiyǒu yìhé suānnǎi, wǒ jiù bǎ suānnǎi hēdiào le.

B: There was still a yogurt in the refrigerator. So I ate the yogurt.

A: Nǐ hēde shì wǒde suānnǎi!

A: What you ate was my yogurt!

B: Wǒ hēde nèihé suānnǎi shì wǒ zìjǐ mǎide, búshì nǐde.

B: The yogurt that I ate was what I bought myself. It was not yours.

A: Nà wǒde suānnǎi bèi shéi hēle ne?

A: In that case, who ate my yogurt?

B: Shàngge xīngqī yī, wǒ xiàlekè, huídào sùshè, kàndào Xiǎo Dīng zài hē suānnǎi. Tā bǎ xiāngjiāo fàngzài suānnǎi lǐ, tā shuō hǎochī jíle.

B: Last Monday, when I came back to the dorm after classes, I saw Xiao Ding eating yogurt. He put the bananas into the yogurt. He said it was extremely delicious.

盒		hé	n./m.w.	box; a box of
酸奶		suānnǎi	n.	yogurt
买	買	mǎi	v.	to buy
被		bèi	aux.	passive voice marker

B：冰箱里还有一盒酸奶，我就把酸奶喝掉了。

A：你喝的是我的酸奶！

B：我喝的那盒酸奶是我自己买的，不是你的。

A：那我的酸奶被谁喝了呢？

B：上个星期一，我下了课，回到宿舍，看到小丁在喝酸奶。他把香蕉放在酸奶里，他说好吃极了。

回		huí	v.	to return, to go back to
宿舍		sùshè	n.	dorm
在		zài	adv.	progressive marker
adj.极了	……極了	… jíle	phrase	extremely …

****

A: Xiǎo Dīng, nǐ zěnme zǒngshì chī wǒde dōngxi?

C: Wǒ bù zhīdào nàshì nǐde dōngxi. Wǒ yǐwéi shì wǒ zìjǐ mǎide.

A: Nǐ lián zìjǐ mǎile shénme dōngxi dōu bù zhīdào ma?!

C: Nǐde kělè hé wǒde kělè kànqǐlái dōu yíyàng, suǒyǐ wǒ jiù bǎ nà sānpíng kělè dōu hēdiào le. Duìbuqǐ.

A: Yǐhòu wǒmen dōu bǎ zìjǐ de míngzi xiě zài zìjǐ de dōngxi shang.

C: Zhèige bànfǎ hǎo shì hǎo, kěshì tài máfan le.

A: Xiǎo Dīng, nǐ yǐjīng hěnpàng le. Yàoshì nǐ zài chī biérén de dōngxi, jiù lián lù dōu zǒubúdòng le!

****

A: Xiao Ding, how come you always eat my stuff?

C: I didn't know that was your stuff. I thought I bought it myself.

A: You don't even know what stuff you bought yourself?!

C: Your cola and my cola look the same; therefore I drank up all those three bottles of cola. I am sorry.

A: In the future let's write our names on our own stuff.

C: Although this method is good, it is too troublesome.

A: Xiao Ding, you are already very fat. If you continue eating other people's stuff, you won't even be able to walk anymore!

知道		zhīdào	v.	to know
连……都 V.P.	連……都 V.P.	lián … dōu	conj.	even …
看起来	看起來	kànqǐlái	phrase	to look like
对不起	對不起	duìbuqǐ	phrase	(I am) sorry

****

A：小丁，你怎么总是吃我的东西？

C：我不知道那是你的东西，我以为是我自己买的。

A：你连自己买了什么东西都不知道吗？

C：你的可乐和我的可乐看起来都一样，所以我就把那三瓶可乐都喝掉了。对不起。

A：以后我们都把自己的名字写在自己的东西上。

C：这个办法好是好，可是太麻烦了。

A：小丁，你已经很胖了。要是你再吃别人的东西，就连路都走不动了！

办法	辦法	bànfǎ	n.	method
麻烦	麻煩	máfán	adj.	troublesome
已经	已經	yǐjīng	adv.	already
胖		pàng	adj.	fat
再		zài	adv.	again; any more
别人		biérén	n.	other people
路		lù	n.	road
走		zǒu	v.	to walk
走不动	走不動	zǒubúdòng	v.c.	not to be able to walk

语法 Grammar Notes

1. 是……的

是……的 is used in sentences of past events to emphasize time, location, and manner of the action. The elements to be emphasized are put between 是 and 的。 When the subject is the emphatic element, the structure goes:

是 subject V.P. 的   It is A who/that …

Lesson 18 elaborates on how the structure can be used to emphasize other parts of the sentence.

▶ 是小丁吃的。
It is Xiao Ding who ate them.

饼干是王老师买的。
It was Teacher Wang who bought the cookies.

2. Verb Complement 掉

掉, used as verb complement, means "finished" and emphasizes the disappearance/removal of the object. In most cases, it is interchangeable with 完.

Verb complement	Potential form	Resultative form
吃掉 eat up	吃得掉 / 吃不掉	吃掉了 / 没吃掉
喝掉 drink up	喝得掉 / 喝不掉	喝掉了 / 没喝掉
用掉 use up	用得掉 / 用不掉	用掉了 / 没用掉

3. 把 Structure (continued)

In Lesson 8, we discussed the use of 把 structure when the status of the object has been changed through the subject's action. The change of status is expressed through a resultative verb complement.

Subject + 把 + object + verb + complement

▶ 我把三瓶可乐都喝掉了。
I drank all three bottles of cola.

他把我的香蕉吃掉了。

He ate my bananas.

The other use of the 把 structure is when the location of an object has been changed through the subject's action. Verb 放 (fàng, to put) is often used in such cases.

Subject + 把 + **object** + **verb** + 在/到 + **location**
(在/到 introduces the new location of the object.)

▶ 以后我们都把自己的名字写在自己的东西上。

In the future we will all write our names on our own stuff.

▶ 他把香蕉放在酸奶里。

He put the bananas into the yogurt.

4. Passive Voice Marker 被

To make a sentence in the passive voice, one can use 被 in the following pattern:

Receiver of action + 被 (+ **doer of action**) + **verb** + **other elements**

The doer of action is optional; therefore it is in parentheses.

▶ 酸奶被你喝掉了。

The yogurt was drunk up by you.

我的书被放到桌子上了。

My book was put on the desk (by somebody).

All adverbs should come immediately before 被.

可乐都被小丁喝了。

All the cola has been drunk by Xiao Ding.

酸奶已经被放到冰箱里了。

The yogurt has already been put into the refrigerator.

In most cases, a passive sentence with 被 can be changed to active voice by using 把. If the doer of the action is missing in the passive voice, one has to add it when changing the sentence into active voice. The above two examples can be reorganized like this:

小丁把可乐都喝了。
Xiao Ding drank all the cola.

他已经把酸奶放到冰箱里了。

He has already put the yogurt into the refrigerator.

5. Subject 在 + V.P.

Progressive marker 在 goes before a verb to indicate that an action is in progress or in a continuous state.

▶ 我在吃饭。
I am eating.

我看到小丁在喝酸奶。
I saw Xiao Ding eating yogurt.

学生在上课。
The students are having class.

6. Modifiers of Adjectives/Stative Verbs

adj. + 极了   extremely
真 + adj.   really

漂亮极了 extremely beautiful   真漂亮 really beautiful
聪明极了 extremely clever   真聪明 really clever
好吃极了 extremely delicious   真好吃 really delicious

Compare to 很:

很，真的, and 极了 show a rank of rising degree in meaning when they modify an adjective respectively. Grammatically speaking, 真 functions similarly to a stressed 很 in that it modifies an adjective functioning as a predicate. In the "adj. + 极了" pattern, 极了 also modifies the adjective/stative verb, but unlike 很 or 真, it follows the adjective, acting as a complement to the adjective/stative verb.

7. V. 起来 + Adj.

Verbs used in this pattern are usually sense verbs such as 看，听，吃, and so on.

看起来   it looks ...
听起来   it sounds ...
吃起来   it tastes ...

▶ 你的可乐和我的可乐看起来都一样。
Your cola and mine look the same.

这家饭馆的饭看起来很好吃，可是吃起来不太好。
The dishes at this restaurant look very tasty, but they don't taste very good.

8. 对不起 (I am sorry)

对不起 has a much narrower meaning in Chinese than what "I am sorry" can express in English. 对不起 indicates only apology and doesn't convey a sense of regret. For example, if you heard that a friend was injured in a car accident, you wouldn't say 对不起 unless it was you who caused the injury and you wanted to apologize.

9. Subject 已经 + V.P. 了 (already)

已经 often pairs with 了, which indicates completion of the action.

▶ 你已经很胖了。
You are already very fat.

我的妹妹已经有男朋友了。
My younger sister has already had a boyfriend.

10. Subject 再 V.P.1, 就 V.P.2 了

If the subject continues doing something, he/she will …

This is an "if" deleted sentence. The adverb 再 here not only means doing something again and again, or continuing to do something, but also has the connotation of "if." The second clause expresses the pending result of the repetitive action by using "就V.P.了" construction. The subject is movable. It can be at the beginning of the first or of the second clause. Moreover, the two clauses may have different subjects.

▶ 要是你再吃别人的东西，连路都走不动了！
If you continue eating other people's stuff, you won't even be able to walk any more.

你再不来，我就把饭都吃掉了。
If you still don't come, I will eat up all the food.

11. 连……都 V.P. (even)

连, means "including," and is paired with 都 to mean "even." The element after 连 usually indicates an extreme exception. The two commonly used patterns are:

Subject 连 object 都 verb

连 subject 都 verb

▶ 小丁连路都走不动了。
Xiao Ding is not even able to walk.

▶ 个中国字太难了，连老师都不会写。
This Chinese character is too difficult, even the teacher can't write it.

Traditional Character Text

誰吃了我的東西

（A——張三，B——李四，C——丁一）

A：我放在冰箱裏的三瓶可樂和兩包餅乾怎麼都不見了呢？

B：我沒吃你的東西。

A：肯定是小丁吃的。

B：上個星期他把我的蘋果、橘子、香蕉和漢堡包都吃掉了。

A：小丁把你的中飯吃掉了，那你吃什麼呢？

B：冰箱裏還有一盒酸奶，我就把酸奶喝掉了。

A：你喝的是我的酸奶！

B：我喝的那盒酸奶是我自己買的，不是你的。

A：那我的酸奶被誰喝了呢？

B：上個星期一，我下了課，回到宿舍，看到小丁在喝酸奶。他把香蕉放在酸奶裏，他說好吃極了。

****

A：小丁，你怎麼總是吃我的東西呢？

C：我不知道那是你的東西，我以為是我自己買的。

A：你連自己買了什麼東西都不知道嗎？

C：你的可樂和我的可樂看起來都一樣，所以我就把那三瓶可樂都喝掉了。對不起。

A：以後我們都把自己的名字寫在自己的東西上。

C：這個辦法好是好，可是太麻煩了。

A：小丁，你已經很胖了。要是你再吃別人的東西，就連路都走不動了。

12

Mén Suǒzhe, Jìnbúqù
(The Door Is Locked, I Cannot Get In)

Pinyin Text

(A—Dīng Yī, B—fúwùyuán, C—Zhāng Sān)

A: Wéi, qǐngwèn fúwùyuán zài ma?

B: Wǒ jiùshì fúwùyuán, nǐ yǒushìr ma?

A: Wǒ de sùshè yàoshi diūle, mén suǒzhe, jìnbúqù. Bù zhīdào néngbunéng máfan nín lái gěiwǒ kāimén.

B: Duìbuqǐ, wǒ xiànzài zhèngzài chīfàn, guòbúqù. Nǐ zhù zài jǐlóu a?

A: Wǒ zhù zài yīlóu.

B: Zhù zài yīlóu, nǐ jiù pá chuānghu jìnqu ba.

English Translation

(A—Ding Yi, B—dorm assistant, C—Zhang San)

A: Hello, may I ask if the [dorm] assistant is there?

B: This is the [dorm] assistant. Can I help you with anything?

A: I lost the dorm key. The door is locked and I cannot get in. I don't know if I can trouble you to open the door for me.

B: I am sorry. I am having my meal right now and cannot go over. On which floor are you staying?

A: I'm staying on the first floor.

B: If you are staying on the first floor, you can climb in through the window.

门	門	mén	n.	door
锁着	鎖著	suǒzhe	adj.	locked
进去	進去	jìnqù	v.c.	to go in
服务员	服務員	fúwùyuán	n.	assistant
事（儿）		shì	n.	matter
钥匙	鑰匙	yàoshi	n.	key
丢了		diūle	v.c.	lost something
能		néng	aux.	can

第十二课 门锁着，进不去

（A——丁一，B——服务员，C——张三）

A：喂，请问服务员在吗？

B：我就是服务员，你有事儿吗？

A：我的宿舍钥匙丢了，门锁着，进不去。不知道能不能麻烦您来给我开门。

B：对不起，我现在正在吃饭，过不去。你住在几楼啊？

A：我住在一楼。

B：住在一楼，你就爬窗户进去吧。

麻烦	麻烦	máfán	v.	to trouble somebody
开门	開門	kāimén	v.o.	to open the door
正在		zhèngzài	adv.	progressive marker
过去	過去	guòqu	v.c.	to go over
住		zhù	v.	to live, to stay
楼	樓	lóu	n.	floor (of a building)
爬		pá	v.	to climb, to crawl
窗户		chuānghù	n.	window

A: Wǒ hěn pàng, chuānghu tài gāo le, wǒ pá bú shàngqù.

B: Chuānghu bùgāo, nǐ xiān ná zhāng zhuōzi, zài bǎ yǐzi fàngzài zhuōzi shang, ránhòu nǐ zhàn zài yǐzi shang, jiù néng pá jìnqu le.

A: Chuānghu hěnxiǎo, wǒ bù zhīdào néng-bunéng pá jìnqù.

B: Nǐ xiān shìshikàn ba. Yàoshì pá bú jìnqù, zài dǎ diànhuà gěi wǒ, wǒ lái bāng nǐde máng.

A: Hǎoba. Xièxie.

****

C: Wéi, shì fúwùyuán ma?

B: Shì, wǒ shì fúwùyuán. Yǒushìr ma?

C: Wǒ shì Xiǎo Dīng de péngyou Xiǎo Zhāng. Tā gāngcái xiǎng cóng chuānghu pájìn wūzi lǐ qù, kěshì tàipàng le, pá bú jìnqù, bù xiǎoxīn cóng yǐzi shang shuāi xiàlái le.

A: I am very heavy, and the window is too high. I cannot climb up.

B: The window is not high. First you grab a table, then put a chair on the table, after that you stand on the chair, and you can climb in.

A: The window is very small. I don't know if I can climb in.

B: Try it first. If you cannot climb in, then give me a call, and I will come over to help you.

A: OK, all right. Thanks.

****

C: Hello, is that the assistant?

B: Yes, this is the assistant. How can I help you?

C: This is Xiao Zhang, Xiao Ding's friend. He wanted to climb into the room from the window just now, but he was too fat to climb in. He fell from the chair out of carelessness.

A：我很胖，窗户太高了，我爬不上去。

B：窗户不高，你先拿张桌子，再把椅子放在桌子上，然后你站在椅子上，就能爬进去了。

A：窗户很小，我不知道能不能爬进去。

B：你先试试看吧，要是爬不进去，再打电话给我，我来帮你的忙。

A：好吧，谢谢。

****

C：喂，是服务员吗？

B：是，我是服务员。有事儿吗？

C：我是小丁的朋友小张。他刚才想从窗户爬进屋子里去，可是太胖了，爬不进去，不小心从椅子上摔下来了。

拿		ná	v.	to grab, to take
然后	然後	ránhòu	conj.	then
站		zhàn	v.	to stand
试	試	shì	v.	to try
帮	幫	bāng	v.	to help
帮somebody的忙		bāng … de máng	v.o.	to do somebody a favor
(不)小心		(bù) xiǎoxīn	adj.	(not) careful
摔		shuāi	v.	to fall

Tā bǎ tuǐ shuāishāng le, yě bǎ chuānghu dǎpò le. Qǐng nǐ jiào yíliàng jiùhùchē, wǒmen děi sòngtā qù yīyuàn.

He hurt his leg and also broke the window. Please get an ambulance. We have to send him to the hospital.

B: Wǒmen zhège hútòngr hěnzhǎi, bù zhīdào jiùhùchē kāide jìnlái kāi bú jìnlái.

B: The alley that we are in is very narrow. I don't know if the ambulance can be driven in or not.

****

****

B: Wéi, shì Xiǎo Zhāng ma? Jiùhùchē kāi jìnlái le. Xiǎo Dīng ne?

B: Hello, is this Xiao Zhang? We have driven the ambulance in. Where is Xiao Ding?

C: Xiǎo Dīng tǎng zài dìshang.

C: Xiao Ding is lying on the ground.

B: Bié dānxīn, wǒmen mǎshàng jiù dào.

B: Don't worry. We will be there right away.

摔伤	摔傷	shuāishāng	v.c.	to fall and get hurt
打		dǎ	v.	to hit, to beat
打破		dǎpò	v.c.	to hit and break
叫		jiào	v.	to call
辆	輛	liàng	m.w.	measure word for vehicles
救护车	救護車	jiùhùchē	n.	ambulance
送		sòng	v.	to send
医院	醫院	yīyuàn	n.	hospital

他把腿摔伤了，也把窗户打破了。请你叫一辆救护车，我
们得送他去医院。

B：我们这个胡同儿很窄，不知道救护车开得进来开不进来。

****

B：喂，是小张吗？救护车开进来了。小丁呢？

C：小丁躺在地上。

B：别担心，我们马上就到。

胡同儿		hútòngr	n.	alley, bystreet
窄		zhǎi	adj.	narrow
开	開	kāi	v.	to drive
躺		tǎng	v.	to lie down
地		dì	n.	floor, ground
别		bié	adv.	don't do something
担心	擔心	dānxīn	v.	to worry
马上	馬上	mǎshàng	adv.	right away
到		dào	v.	to arrive

语法 Grammar Notes

1. Directional Complements

Directional complements are a category of verb complements that tell the direction in which the action of a verb moves. Directional complements can be simple or compound.

(1) Simple Directional Complements

V + 来 and V + 去 are the two simple directional complements. Both 来 and 去 can be used as a verb, meaning "to come" and "to go," respectively. Based on their meaning as a main verb, when they are used as directional complements, 来 indicates that the action moves toward the speaker and 去 indicates that the action moves away from the speaker. The speaker's standpoint is the decisive factor that determines the choice between 来 and 去.

> V + 来 (toward the speaker)
> V + 去 (away from the speaker)

▶ 门锁着，我进不去。
The door is locked, and I can't get in.

▶ 我现在正在吃饭，过不去。
I am eating right now, and I can't go over.

The underlined phrases in the above two examples from the text are the negative potential form of the simple directional complements.

Examples of simple directional complements are given below:

Due to the speaker's position	
V 来	V 去
进来 to come in	进去 to go in
下来 to come down	下去 to go down
上来 to come up	上去 to go up
过来 to come over	过去 to go over
回来 to come back	回去 to go back
出来 to come out	出去 to go out

(2) Compound Directional Complements

In compound directional complements, a simple directional complement follows the main verb:

main verb + **V.** + 来/去

↓

Simple Directional Complement

Main verb: the main verb can be any verb that involves movement in a direction. For example: 走 (zǒu, to walk), 跑 (pǎo, to run), 跳 (tiào, to jump), 摔 (shuāi, to fall), 躺 (tǎng, to lie down), 坐 (zuò, to sit), 开 (kāi, to drive), and so on.

Examples of compound directional complements from this text are given below.

▶ 窗户太高了，我怕爬不上去。
The window is too high; I am afraid that I can't climb up.

▶ 站在椅子上，你就能爬进去了。
Standing on the chair, you will be able to climb in.

▶ 他从椅子上摔下来了。
He fell down from the chair.

▶ 救护车开进来了。
The ambulance drove in.

Note:

(a) Both simple and compound directional complements are usually pronounced in neutral tones.

(b) In some exceptional cases for the compound directional complements, 来 or 去 can be omitted. For example, 坐下 (sit down).

(c) If the destination of the movement needs to be indicated, it can be inserted between the verb and the directional complement.

Simple directional complement:

V. + destination + complement

Compound directional complement:

main verb + **V. + destination + complement**

(simple directional complement)

▶ 他想爬进屋子里去。
He wanted to climb into the room.

In this sentence, the destination of his action (to climb) is the room 屋子. It is inserted between 进 and 去.

(3) Potential and Resultative Directional Complements

All directional complements have potential forms and resultative forms.

For the potential form, 得 is used to indicate "can," or 不 to indicate "cannot."

For simple directional complements, 得/不 comes between the verb and 来/去.

For compound directional complements, 得/不 comes between the main verb and the simple directional complement.

		Base	Potential form positive	Potential form negative	Potential form question
Toward the speaker	Simple directional complements	进来	进得来	进不来	进得来进不来
	Compound directional complements	爬进来	爬得进来	爬不进来	爬得进来爬不进来
Away from the speaker	Simple directional complements	进去	进得去	进不去	进得去进不去
	Compound directional complements	爬进去	爬得进去	爬不进去	爬得进去爬不进去

For the resultative form, 了 is added at the end of all directional complements to indicate completion of the action as the result, 没/没有 is added at the beginning of all directional complements to indicate the failure of the action.

		Base	Potential form positive	Potential form negative	Potential form question
Toward the speaker	Simple directional complements	进来	进来了	没进来	进来了没有 or 进来了吗
	Compound directional complements	爬进来	爬进来了	没爬进来	爬进来了没有 or 爬进来了吗
Away from the speaker	Simple directional complements	进去	进去了	没进去	进去了没有 or 进去了吗
	Compound directional complements	爬进去	爬进去了	没爬进去	爬进去了没有 or 爬进去了吗

2. Auxiliary Verb 能 (can, be able to)

Although the auxiliary verbs 能 and 会 (see Lesson 6, note 4) are both translated as "can, be able to" in English, they have quite different uses and connotations in Chinese. 会 emphasizes the ability or skill to do something acquired through learning. Skills with language is a typical example in which one uses 会：

我会说中文，也会写中国字。
I can speak Chinese, and I can also write Chinese characters.

能 (negative form 不能， question form 能不能) is often used in the following two situations:

(1) In the sense of being allowed without prevention

你能不能给我开门？ Can you open the door for me?
你能不能帮我的忙？ Can you do me a favor?

(2) In the sense of "to have the physical ability to do"

他把腿摔伤了，所以不能走路。
He broke his leg, therefore he can't walk (it is not that he doesn't know how to walk, but he can't walk due to physical restrictions).
我不能吃苹果。
I can't eat apples (due to physical reasons, such as an allergy).

3. 麻烦 Somebody V.P. (to trouble somebody to do something)

When used in a request, as in the examples below, 麻烦 softens the tone and indicates politeness.

▶ 能不能麻烦您帮我开门？
May I trouble you to open the door for me?

我能不能麻烦您帮我叫一辆车？
May I trouble you to help me get a car?

4. 给 Somebody V.P.

The preposition 给 has two meanings:

(1) For somebody, that is, to provide service for or for the benefit of somebody

▶ 给我开门　　　 to open the door for me
给朋友买东西　 to buy stuff for friends

(2) To somebody

A typical example is the phrase "to call somebody":

给 somebody 打电话　　　or

打电话给 somebody

▶ 要是爬不进去，再打电话给我。

If you cannot climb in, then give me a call.

5. V.V. 看 (to try to do something)

Verbs that appear in this phrase are restricted to monosyllabic verbs. Except for the verb 看 itself, because of redundancy, almost all other monosyllabic verbs can be combined with 看 to express the meaning of trying to do something.

▶ 你先试试看吧。

Why don't you try it first?

这家饭馆儿的牛排很好，你吃吃看。

This restaurant's steak is very good. Try it.

6. Review: 把 Structure

Subject 把 + definite object + resultative complement

In this pattern, the changes to the object caused by the subject's action are emphasized, since the resultative complement comes after the object.

▶ 他把腿摔伤了。

He broke his leg.

▶ 他把窗户打破了。

He broke the window.

Note: In English, both of the above sentences use the verb "broke." However, in Chinese, a different verb is used in each sentence due to the different objects.

7. 住 (to live, to stay)

The special feature of the verb 住 is that the adverbial modifier about location (在 + place word) can go either before or after 住.

在 + p.w. + 住

住 + 在 + p.w.

This contradicts our earlier rule that location precedes action. The reason for such exceptional flexibility with 住 is because it is a nonaction, status verb. In this lesson, two other verbs, 躺 (to lie down) and 站 (to stand), and 长 (to grow) from Lesson 10 all fall into the same category.

躺在地上　　　to lie on the floor
站在桌子上　　to stand on the desk

To emphasize the continuing state, the progressive suffix 着 is customarily added after the verb. When using 着, the location has to precede the verb 躺 and 站.

在地上躺着　　lying on the floor
在桌子上站着　standing on the desk

8. 送 Somebody + V.P. (to accompany/send somebody to do something or to some place)

▶ 请你叫一辆救护车，我们得送他去医院。
Please get an ambulance. We have to send him to the hospital.

我的朋友送我回家。
My friends accompany me home.

Note that in the phrase "叫一辆救护车" the verb 叫 is used to mean getting (a car). Similar expressions include 叫一辆出租车 (chūzū chē), which means "to get a taxi."

9. Subject 马上就 V.P.(了)

This structure indicates the action is about to take place. 了 used at the end of the sentence indicates change of status, and it is optional.

▶ 我们马上就到。
We will be there right away.

他马上就出去了。
He was about to go out right away.

10. 别 + V.P. (Don't do ...)

This construction is usually used in imperative sentences.

▶ 别担心。
Don't worry.

晚上别喝咖啡。
Don't drink coffee at night.

Traditional Character Text

門鎖着，進不去

（A——丁一，B——服務員，C——張三）

A：喂，請問服務員在嗎？

B：我就是服務員，你有事兒嗎？

A：我的宿舍鑰匙丟了，門鎖着，進不去。不知道能不能麻煩您來給我開門。

B：對不起，我現在正在吃飯，過不去。你住在幾樓啊？

A：我住在一樓。

B：住在一樓，你就爬窗戶進去吧。

A：我很胖，窗戶太高了，我爬不上去。

B：窗戶不高，你先拿張桌子，再把椅子放在桌子上，然後你站在椅子上，就能爬進去了。

A：窗戶很小，我不知道能不能爬進去。

B：你先試試看吧。要是爬不進去，再打電話給我，我來幫你的忙。

A：好吧。謝謝。

****

C：喂，是服務員嗎？

B：是，我是服務員，有事兒嗎？

C：我是小丁的朋友小張。他剛才想從窗戶爬進屋子裏去，可是太胖了，爬不進去，不小心從椅子上摔下來了。他把腿摔傷了，也把窗戶打破了。請你叫一輛救護車，我們得送他去醫院。

B：我們這個胡同儿很窄，不知道救護車開得進來開不進來。

****

B：喂，是小張嗎？救護車開進來了。小丁呢？

C：小丁躺在地上。

B：別擔心，我們馬上就到。

13 Mǎixié (Buy Shoes)

Pinyin Text

(A—shòuhuòyuán, B—gùkè)

A: Qǐngwèn, nín xiǎng mǎi shénme xié?

B: Wǒ xiǎng mǎi shuāng lánsè de qiúxié.

A: Nín chuān jǐhào de xié?

B: Wǒ chuān bāhào bàn de xié.

A: Wǒmen méiyǒu bāhào bàn de lánsè qiúxié, zhǐyǒu bāhào de hé jiǔhào de.

B: Qǐng nǐ bǎ bāhào de hé jiǔhào de dōu nálái ràng wǒ shìshi ba.

A: Zhèishuāng shì bāhào de, nín shìshi.

B: Bāhào de yǒuyìdiǎnr xiǎo, wǒ chuān bú jìnqù. Yǒu dà yìdiǎnr de ma?

A: Zhèishuāng shì jiǔhào de, bǐ bāhào de dà yìdiǎnr, nín zài shìshi.

B: Jiǔhào de bǐ bāhào de dà duōle, chuān qǐlái bù shūfu.

English Translation

(A—shop assistant, B—customer)

A: May I ask what kind of shoes you want to buy?

B: I want to buy a pair of blue sneakers.

A: What size do you wear?

B: I wear size eight and a half.

A: We don't have blue sneakers in size eight and a half. We only have size eight and size nine.

B: Please bring me both size eight and size nine and let me try them on.

A: This pair is size eight, please try them.

B: Size eight is a bit small. I can't put them on. Do you have a bigger size?

A: This pair is size nine. It's a little bigger than size eight. Please try them again.

B: Size nine is much bigger than size eight. This pair feels uncomfortable.

售货员	售貨員	shòuhuòyuán	n.	shop assistant
顾客	顧客	gùkè	n.	customer
鞋		xié	n.	shoes
双	雙	shuāng	m.w.	a pair of (shoes, socks, chopsticks)
蓝色	藍色	lánsè	n.	blue color

第十三课 买鞋

（A——售货员，B——顾客）

A：请问，您想买什么鞋？

B：我想买双蓝色的球鞋。

A：您穿几号的鞋？

B：我穿8号半的鞋。

A：我们没有8号半的蓝色球鞋，只有8号的和9号的。

B：请你把8号的和9号的都拿来让我试试吧。

A：这双是8号的，您试试。

B：8号的有一点儿小，我穿不进去。有大一点儿的吗？

A：这双是9号的，比8号的大一点儿，您再试试。

B：9号的比8号的大多了，穿起来不舒服。

球鞋		qiúxié	n.	sneakers
穿		chuān	v.	to wear, to put on (clothes/shoes)
号	號	hào	n.	size
半		bàn	n.	half
让	讓	ràng	v.	to let, to make
舒服		shūfu	adj.	comfortable

A: Qíshí bāhào de hé jiǔhào de chàbuduō yíyàng dà, bìng méiyǒu hěndà de bùtóng. Nín yào shìshi biéde yánsè ma?

B: Hǎoba, wǒ xiǎng kànkan báisè de.

A: Zhè shì tóng yíge páizi, bāhào bàn de báisè qiúxié.

B: Dàxiǎo hěn héshì, kěshì báisè de méiyǒu lánsè de nàme hǎokàn. Zhèishuāng xié duōshǎo qián?

A: Jīntiān wǒmen dǎ bāzhé, zhèi shuāng xié zhǐyào qīshíjiǔ kuài jiǔmáo jiǔ.

B: Suīrán búguì, kěshì yàngzi hé yánsè bútài hǎokàn. Nǐ yǒu hēisè de qiúxié ma?

A: Yǒu, yǒu, yǒu! Hēisè de bǐjiào guì, xiànzài bù dǎzhé.

A: Actually size eight and size nine are about the same. There isn't a big difference. Do you want to try some other colors?

B: Okay. I would like to see the white ones.

A: This is the same brand, white sneakers in size eight and a half.

B: They do fit well, but the white pair isn't as good-looking as the blue one. How much is this pair of shoes?

A: We have a twenty percent off sale today. This pair of shoes is only $79.99.

B: Although they are not expensive, the style and color aren't very nice. Do you have black sneakers?

A: Yes, we do. The black pair is relatively more expensive. They're not on sale.

其实	其實	qíshí	adv.	actually, in fact
差不多		chàbuduō	adj./adv.	similar; almost, nearly
要		yào	v.	to want
别的		biéde	adj.	other
颜色	顏色	yánsè	n.	color
白色		báisè	n.	white color
同一 +m.w.+ n.		tóng yī	phrase	the same …
牌子		páizi	n.	brand

A：其实8号的和9号的差不多一样大，并没有很大的不同。您要试试别的颜色的吗？

B：好吧，我想看看白色的。

A：这是同一个牌子，8号半的白色球鞋。

B：大小很合适，可是白色的没有蓝色的那么好看。这双鞋多少钱？

A：今天我们打8折，这双鞋只要79块9毛9。

B：虽然不贵，可是样子和颜色不太好看。你有黑色的球鞋吗？

A：有，有，有！黑色的比较贵，现在不打折。

大小		dàxiǎo	n.	size
合适	合適	héshì	adj.	suitable
好看		hǎokàn	adj.	good-looking
多少		duōshǎo	q.w.	how much, how many
钱	錢	qián	n.	money
打折		dǎzhé	v.	to be on sale, to have a discount
块	塊	kuài	m.w.	(currency unit) dollar or yuan
毛		máo	m.w.	(currency unit) ten cents
样子	樣子	yàngzi	n.	appearance, style
比较	比較	bǐjiào	adv.	relatively
贵	貴	guì	adj.	expensive

B: Hēixié bǐ báixié guì duōshǎo qián?

A: Hēixié bǐ báixié guì èrshí kuài qián, báixié bǐ hēixié piányi èrshí kuài qián. Qíshí, hēixié gēn báixié wánquán yíyàng, méiyǒu shénme bùtóng. Nín jiù mǎi báixié ba.

B: Hǎoba, wǒ néng yòng xìnyòngkǎ ma?

A: Duìbuqǐ, nín zhǐnéng yòng xiànjīn.

B: Zhè shì yìbǎi kuài qián.

A: Zhǎo nín èrshí kuài. Xièxie!

B: Bú kèqi. Zàijiàn!

A: Zàijiàn!

B: How much more are the black shoes than the white shoes?

A: The black pair is twenty dollars more than the white pair. The white pair is twenty dollars less than the black pair. Actually, the black shoes and the white shoes are exactly the same. There isn't any difference. Why don't you buy the white shoes?

B: Okay. Can I use credit card?

A: Sorry, you can only use cash.

B: Here's one hundred dollars.

A: Twenty is your change. Thanks!

B: You're welcome. See you!

A: See you!

便宜		piányi	adj.	inexpensive, cheap
完全		wánquán	adv.	completely
信用卡		xìnyòng kǎ	n.	credit card
现金	现金	xiànjīn	n.	cash
百		bǎi	n.	hundred
找		zhǎo	v.	to give change (of money)
再见		zàijiàn	phrase	good-bye

B：黑鞋比白鞋贵多少钱？

A：黑鞋比白鞋贵20块钱，白鞋比黑鞋便宜20块钱。其实，
　　黑鞋跟白鞋完全一样，没有什么不同。您就买白鞋吧。

B：好吧，我能用信用卡吗？

A：对不起，您只能用现金。

B：这是一百块钱。

A：找您20块。谢谢！

B：不客气。再见！

A：再见！

语法 Grammar Notes

1. Colors

Color can be translated as sè 色 or yánsè 颜色 in Chinese. The colors that we have learned so far include hóngsè 红色 (red) , lánsè 蓝色 (blue), báisè 白色 (white), hēisè 黑色 (black), and lǜsè 绿色 (green). Other common colors are huángsè 黄色 (yellow), zōngsè 棕色 (brown), zǐsè 紫色 (purple), fěnhóngsè 粉红色 (pink), and huīsè 灰色 (gray).

The following is the pattern to describe the color of something, and 色 is optional.

> **Subject** 是 + **color** + 的。

> ▶ 中文书是红的，英文书是蓝的。
> The Chinese book is red, and the English book is blue.

> 这本书是红色的。
> This book is red.

2. Talking about Price

The most basic units for Chinese money are 元 yuán (Chinese dollar), 角 jiǎo (10 cents), and 分 fēn (cent); the more colloquial equivalents are 块 kuài, 毛 máo, and 分 fēn.

¥ X	X元 or X块
¥ X.Y	X元Y角 or X块Y毛 (角 and 毛 are optional)
¥ X.YZ	X元Y角Z分 or X块Y毛Z分 (分 is optional)

The simplest way to ask for price is:

> **X** 多少钱？

> ▶A: 这双鞋多少钱？　　How much is this pair of shoes?
> B: 这双鞋只要79.99。　This pair is only $79.99.

Note: 只要/只有 + amount: only ...

3. 让 Someone + Verb (+ object) 吧！(Let someone do something!)

This is an imperative sentence, and the particle 吧 is attached to the end of the sentence to signal a request or a suggestion. Its presence often softens the tone.

> 黑色的和白色的球鞋都让我试试吧！
> Let me try both the black and the white sneakers!

让那个学生坐在前边儿吧！
Let that student sit in the front!

4. 其实 (adv./insertion) (actually, in fact)

其实 is used to correct a mistaken opinion. It is sometimes preceded by a clause with 以为, which expresses an earlier and mistaken opinion. It can be placed at the front of a sentence as an insertion or between the subject and the verb.

Subject 以为……，其实……

Subject thought … , but actually …

▶ 其实，黑鞋跟白鞋完全一样。
Actually, the black shoes and the white shoes are completely the same.

我以为中国的东西都很便宜，其实有的东西比美国的还贵。
I thought that things in China are all cheap, but in fact, some things are even more expensive than those in the United States.

5. Review: Comparison

A 比 B + adj. (+ complement)

The preposition 比 is used to make a comparison between two items, A and B. The adjective must be in its original form and cannot take any modifier such as 很. A complement of degree can be added after the adjective to provide further information. Complements that are commonly used include:

(1) A 比 B + adj. 一点儿   A is a little more adj. than B

Even though sometimes "比 B" does not appear in the sentence, "adj. 一点儿" always implies comparison with something else. This implicit comparison form is different from another pattern, "有一点儿 adj.," which usually implies excessiveness and means "a bit too adj."

▶ 8号的有一点儿小，有大一点儿的吗？
Size eight is a bit too small. Do you have something a little bigger?

这本书有点儿贵。那本便宜一点儿吗？
This book is a little bit expensive. Is that one a little cheaper?

(2) A 比 B + adj. 多了   A is much more adj. than B

▶ 9号的比8号的大多了。
Size nine is much bigger than size eight.

白鞋比黑鞋便宜多了。

White shoes are much cheaper than black shoes.

我写中国字比我的同学快多了。

I write Chinese characters much faster than my classmates.

6. "Sameness" in Comparison

A 和/跟 B (差不多)一样 adj.　　A and B are (about) the same adj.

A 和/跟 B 差不多/一样　　A and B are similar/the same.

A 和/跟 B 没有(很大的/什么)不同　　A is not (very/any) different from B

▶ 其实8号的和9号的差不多一样大。

In fact, size eight is almost as big as size nine.

我的妹妹和我差不多一样高。

My younger sister and I are about the same height.

7. 比较 + adj. (relatively more adj.)

▶ 黑色的比较贵，现在不打折。

The black ones are relatively more expensive; they are not currently on sale.

妹妹没有姐姐那么漂亮，可是比较聪明。

The younger sister is not as pretty as the older sister, but she is relatively smarter.

8. (Clothes/shoes) 穿得进去/穿不进去 (can/cannot fit into)

▶8号的有一点儿小，穿不进去。

Size eight is a bit too small, and (my feet) cannot fit into (the shoes).

妹妹有很多漂亮的鞋，可是我都穿不进去。

My younger sister has a lot of pretty shoes, but I cannot fit into (them).

Traditional Character Text

買鞋

(A——售貨員，B——顧客)

A：請問，您想買什麼鞋？

B：我想買雙藍色的球鞋。

A：您穿幾號的鞋？

B：我穿8號半的鞋。

A：我們沒有8號半的藍色球鞋，只有8號的和9號的。

B：請你把8號的和9號的都拿來讓我試試吧。

A：這雙是8號的，您試試。

B：8號的有一點兒小，我穿不進去。有大一點兒的嗎？

A：這雙是9號的，比8號的大一點兒，您再試試。

B：9號的比8號的大多了，穿起來不舒服。

A：其實8號的和9號的差不多一樣大，並沒有很大的不同。您
要試試別的顏色的嗎？

B：好吧，我想看看白色的。

A：這是同一個牌子，8號半的白色球鞋。

B：大小很合適，可是白色的沒有藍色的那麼好看。這雙鞋多少
錢？

A：今天我們打8折，這雙鞋只要79塊9毛9。

B：雖然不貴，可是樣子和顏色不太好看。你有黑色的球鞋嗎？

A：有，有，有！黑色的比較貴，現在不打折。

B：黑鞋比白鞋貴多少錢？

A：黑鞋比白鞋貴20塊錢，白鞋比黑鞋便宜20塊錢。其實，黑鞋跟白鞋完全一樣，沒有什麼不同。您就買白鞋吧。

B：好吧，我能用信用卡嗎？

A：對不起，您只能用現金。

B：這是一百塊錢。

A：找您20塊。謝謝！

B：不客氣。再見！

A：再見！

CHAPTER 14

Qǐbùlái, Chídàole
(Can't Get Up and Late for School)

Pinyin Text

(A—Zhāng Sān, B—Dīng Yī)

A: Qǐ láile, qǐláile, jiǔdiǎn bàn le! Zài bù qǐlái, yòu yào chídào le!

B: Shénme? Yǐjīng jiǔdiǎn bàn le! Xiànzài qù jiàoshì dōu kuài xiàkè le. Nǐ zěnme bù zǎo diǎnr jiào wǒ?

A: Wǒ yě gāng qǐchuáng, wǒ sāndiǎn cái shuìjiào, tàilèile, qǐbulái.

B: Nǐ zěnme sāndiǎn cái shuìjiào ne?

A: Jīntiān xiàwǔ de lìshǐ kè, wǒ děi zuò bàogào. Wǒ zhǔnbèi dào zǎoshàng sāndiǎn, hái méi zhǔnbèi hǎo ne. Nǐ xiànzài yǒu shénme kè a?

English Translation

(A—Zhang San, B—Ding Yi)

A: Get up, get up. It's already nine thirty! If you still don't get up, you'll be late again.

B: What? Already nine thirty! If I go to the classroom now, class will already be almost over. Why didn't you wake me up earlier?

A: I also just got up. I didn't sleep until three o'clock. I was too tired and couldn't get up.

B: How come you went to bed at three o'clock?

A: I have to do a presentation in history class this afternoon. I was preparing for it till three o'clock in the morning, and I'm still not ready. What class do you have now?

起来	起來	qǐlái	v.	to get up
要		yào	aux.	will
迟到	遲到	chídào	v.	to arrive late
教室		jiàoshì	n.	classroom
都		dōu	adv.	already (colloquial)
下课	下課	xiàkè	v.o.	class is over
早		zǎo	adj.	early
叫		jiào	v.	to call, to wake up
刚	剛	gāng	adv.	just
起床		qǐchuáng	v.o	to get up (from bed)

第十四课 起不来，迟到了

（A——张三，B——丁一）

A：起来了，起来了，九点半了！再不起来，又要迟到了！

B：什么！已经九点半了！现在去教室，都快下课了。你怎么不早点儿叫我？

A：我也刚起床，我三点才睡觉，太累了，起不来。

B：你怎么三点才睡觉呢？

A：今天下午的历史课，我得做报告。我准备到早上三点，还没准备好呢。你现在有什么课啊？

才		cái	adv.	to indicate "later than expected"
睡觉	睡覺	shuìjiào	v.o.	to go to bed, to sleep
累		lèi	adj.	tired
下午		xiàwǔ	n.	afternoon (time word)
报告	報告	bàogào	n.	report, presentation
准备	准備	zhǔnbèi	v.	to prepare

B: Wǒ měitiān zǎoshàng jiǔdiǎn dōu yǒu Zhōngwén kè. Wǒ zuì bù xǐhuān Xīngqīwǔ de Zhōngwén kè, yīnwèi děi bèi kèwén.

A: Wǒ yě bù xǐhuān Xīngqīwǔ de lìshǐ kè, búshì bàogào jiùshì kǎoshì, yìdiǎnr yìsi dōu méiyǒu.

B: Xīngqīwǔ yīnggāi shì zuì qīngsōng de yìtiān, kěshì wǒ juéde shì zuì jǐnzhāng de yìtiān. Wǒ juédìng jīntiān búqù shàngkè le, gěi zìjǐ fàng yìtiān jià.

A: Nǐ chángcháng gěi zìjǐ fàngjià, búpà chéngji yuèláiyuèchà ma?

B: Wǒ juéde jiànkāng bǐ chéngji zhòngyào de duō, měitiān jiǔdiǎn shàngkè, wǒ kěndìng huì shēngbìng.

A: Nǐ zhēnlǎn!

B: I have a Chinese class at nine every morning. I dislike Friday's Chinese class the most, because we have to recite our text.

A: I also don't like Friday's history class. It's either a presentation or an examination, no fun at all.

B: Friday should be the most relaxing day, but I think it's the busiest day. I've decided not to go to class today. I'll give myself one day off.

A: You often give yourself days off. Aren't you worried about your grades getting worse?

B: I think health is much more important than grades. If I go to class at nine every day, I'll certainly get sick.

A: You are really lazy!

课文	課文	kèwén	n.	text of a lesson
背课文	背課文	bèikèwén	v.o.	to recite a text
不是……	就是……	búshì … jiùshì	conj.	if not … then …
应该	應該	yīnggāi	aux v.	should, ought to
轻松	輕鬆	qīngsōng	adj.	relaxed, relaxing
紧张	緊張	jǐnzhāng	adj.	tense, nervous
决定	決定	juédìng	v.	to decide
放假		fàngjià	v.o.	to have a vacation/days off

B：我每天早上九点都有中文课。我最不喜欢星期五的中文课，因为得背课文。

A：我也不喜欢星期五的历史课，不是报告，就是考试，一点儿意思都没有。

B：星期五应该是最轻松的一天，可是我觉得是最紧张的一天。我决定今天不去上课了，给自己放一天假。

A：你常常给自己放假，不怕成绩越来越差吗？

B：我觉得健康比成绩重要得多，每天九点上课，我肯定会生病。

A：你真懒！

怕		pà	v.	to fear; to be afraid of
成绩	成績	chéngjì	n.	academic record, grade
越来越……	越來越……	yuèláiyuè	adv.	more and more …
差		chà	adj.	inferior in quality
健康		jiànkāng	n./adj.	health; healthy
重要		zhòngyào	adj.	important
生病		shēngbìng	v.	to get sick, to fall ill
懒		lǎn	adj.	lazy

语法 Grammar Notes

1. Time Words

Time words are an important class of words that refer to time points or the duration of time. They are nouns, but are frequently used in ways that make them resemble adverbs. They must appear before the verb, but can appear either before or after the subject of a sentence. The time words in this text are 现在, 早上, 下午, 星期五, X点 (indicating the hour of the day), and so on.

▶ 现在去教室，都快下课了！

If I go to the classroom now, class will already be almost over.

我每天早上九点都有中文课。Or 每天早上九点我都有中文课。

I have Chinese class at nine every morning.

2. Time Word + 才 + Verb

才 as an adverb can be understood literally as "only then." It is used between a time word and a verb to indicate that an action happens later than one expected. The meaning is similar to the English expression "not until. …"

▶ 我三点才上床。

I didn't go to bed untill three o'clock.

他们九点有课，可是他九点半才去教室。

They have class at nine, but he didn't go to the classroom until nine thirty.

3. Expressing Hours of the Day

The basic time units are 点 (o'clock) and 分 (minutes).

X o'clock X 点
X o'clock Y minutes X点Y分

Since 30 minutes is half an hour, X o'clock 30 minutes is also X 点半; 刻 (kè) means a quarter of an hour. Therefore, 一刻 is 15 minutes and 三刻 is 45 minutes. 早上 (morning), 上午 (before noon), 中午 (noon), 下午 (afternoon) and 晚上 (evening, night) are often placed before the clock time to show whether the given time is a.m. or p.m.

9:00 p.m.　　晚上九点　　　　　9:00 a.m.　　早上九点

11:15 p.m.	晚上十一点一刻	11:15 a.m.	上午11点一刻
3:30 p.m.	下午三点半	3:30 a.m.	早上三点半
5:10 p.m.	下午五点十分	5:10 a.m.	早上五点十分

When there is more than one time word, follow the order from the larger concept to the smaller concept. This is the opposite of how time is expressed in English. This rule applies also to location. For example:

At 9:00 a.m. Friday morning   星期五早上9点

Beijing, China   中国北京

4. 再 vs. 又

Both 再 and 又 are adverbs and mean "again." While 再 is used to mark the repetition of an action when the repetition has yet to take place, 又 is used to indicate the repetition of an action when the repetition has already taken place.

昨天我去找老师，他不在。我今天又去找他，他又不在。我明天再去找他。

I went to look for the teacher yesterday, and he wasn't there. I went to look for him again today, and he wasn't there either. I'll go and look for him again tomorrow.

Two common structures with 再 and 又 are these:

a. Subject 再 V.P.1, (就) V.P.2 了

If the subject continues doing something, he/she will. …

This is an "if" deleted sentence. The adverb 再 here not only means doing something again and again, or continuing to do something, but also has the connotation of "if." The second clause expresses the pending result of the repetitive action. The position of the subject is movable. It can be at the beginning of the first or the second clause. Moreover, the two clauses may have different subjects.

你再不来，我就把饭都吃掉了。

If you still don't come, I will eat up all the food.

b. 又要 V. 了 something is sure to happen again

▶ 你再不起来，又要迟到了！

If you still don't get up, you'll be late again!

5. 刚 (adv.) (just)

刚 is an adverb that sets the verb it modifies in the immediate past. 刚 never appears before a subject, and usually is not used with the continuous tense (when an action is in progress at the time indicated), while 刚才, as a time word, can be used before the subject and with the continuous tense.

▶ 我也刚起床。
I also just got up.

刚才我在吃饭。我刚吃完饭。
I was eating a while ago. I just finished my meal.

6. 不是 A，就是 B (If not A, then B; either A or B (no other options))

This pattern indicates there are only two options; if it's not option A, then it is option B. These two options are usually habitual actions.

▶ 星期五的历史课不是报告就是考试。
In Friday's history class, if we don't do a presentation, then we'll have an examination.

她的鞋不是黑色就是白色。
Her shoes are either black or white.

7. 一点儿 + Uncountable Noun + 都没有 (not have even a little bit of . ...)

The expression 一点意思都没有 originates from the phrase 有意思 (有意思, "interesting," functioning as an adjective, is a verb + object construction, and literally means "to have meaning"), the negative of which is 没有意思 (not interesting). 一点儿意思都没有 is an emphatic form of the negative.

▶ 星期五的历史课一点儿意思都没有。
Friday's history class is not interesting at all.

杯子里一点儿水都没有。
There is no water at all in the cup.

8. 越来越 + Adj./Emotion Verb (more and more)

越来越…… functions as an adverb indicating the increasing intensity in degree of the adjective or emotion verb following it.

▶ 他的成绩越来越差。
His grade is getting worse and worse.

中文课越来越难，可是我越来越喜欢。
Chinese classes are getting harder and harder, but I like them more and more.

Traditional Character Text

起不來，遲到了

(A——張三，B——丁一)

A：起來了，起來了，九點半了！再不起來，又要遲到了！

B：什麼！已經九點半了！現在去教室，都快下課了。你怎麼不早點兒叫我？

A：我也剛起床，我三點才睡覺，太累了，起不來。

B：你怎麼三點才睡覺呢？

A：今天下午的歷史課，我得做報告。我準備到早上三點，還沒準備好呢。你現在有什麼課啊？

B：我每天早上九點都有中文課。我最不喜歡星期五的中文課，因為得背課文。

A：我也不喜歡星期五的歷史課，不是報告，就是考試，一點兒意思都沒有。

B：星期五應該是最輕鬆的一天，可是我覺得是最緊張的一天。我決定今天不去上課了，給自己放一天假。

A：你常常給自己放假，不怕成績越來越差嗎？

B：我覺得健康比成績重要得多，每天九點上課，我肯定會生病。

A：你真懶！

15 Xiàxuě le (It's Snowing!)

Pinyin Text

(A—Zhāng Sān, B—Dīng Yī)

A: Jīntiān zhème lěng, nǐ zěnme zhǐ chuān yí jiàn chènshān a?

B: Tiānqì lěng shì lěng, kěshì jiàoshì lǐ tǐng nuǎnhuo de, chuānshang máoyī jiù bù shūfu le.

A: Nǐ zhèyàng chūqu, kǒngpà huì gǎnmào.

B: Chūqu de shíhou, chuānshang dàyī, jiù méiyǒu wèntí le.

English Translation

(A—Zhang San, B—Ding Yi)

A: It is so cold today. Why are you only wearing a shirt?

B: Though the weather is cold, it's pretty warm in the classroom. It would not be comfortable to wear a sweater.

A: If you go out like this, I'm afraid you'll catch a cold.

B: There won't be a problem if I put on my overcoat when going out.

下雪		xiàxuě	v.o.	to snow
天气	天氣	tiānqì	n.	weather
这么		zhème	adv.	so, this (adj.)
冷		lěng	adj.	cold
件		jiàn	m.w.	measure word for clothes
衬衫	襯衫	chènshān	n.	shirt
挺 adj./emotion verb 的		tǐng … de	adv.	quite, pretty
暖和		nuǎnhuo	adj.	warm
毛衣		máoyī	n.	sweater
这样	這樣	zhèyàng	phrase	like this, in this way
恐怕		kǒngpà	v.	to be afraid that
感冒		gǎnmào	v./n.	to catch a cold/flu; cold
时候	時候	shíhòu	n.	time when …
大衣		dàyī	n.	overcoat

第十五课 下雪了

（A——张三，B——丁一）

A: 今天这么冷，你怎么只穿一件衬衫啊？

B: 天气冷是冷，可是教室里挺暖和的，穿上毛衣就不舒服了。

A: 你这样出去，恐怕会感冒。

B: 出去的时候，穿上大衣，就没有问题了。

A: Wàitou xiàzhexuě ne, hái búdào èrshí dù. Fēng guā dào liǎnshàng zhēn bù shūfu.

B: Zhèr de tiānqì biànhuà de hěnkuài. Zuótiān hái xiàng xiàtiān, yǒu rén chuān duǎnxiù chènshān hé duǎnkù, jīntiān jiù xià qǐ xuě lái le. Zhèr de xiàtiān rè, dōngtiān lěng, zhǐyǒu chūntiān qiūtiān bǐjiào shūfu. Búguò, sì wǔ yuè chángcháng xiàyǔ. Chūqu de shíhou děi dài yǔsǎn, hěn bù fāngbiàn.

A: It's snowing outside, and it's not even 20 degrees. It feels uncomfortable when the wind blows against your face.

B: The weather here changes quickly. It seemed like summer yesterday, with people wearing short-sleeve shirts and shorts, yet it started to snow today. It's hot in summer and cold in winter. Only in spring and fall is it relatively comfortable. However, it often rains in April and May. You need to take an umbrella with you when you go out. It is very inconvenient.

不到		búdào	phrase	less, fewer than …
度		dù	n.	degree (of temperature)
风	風	fēng	n.	wind
刮		guā	v.	(wind) to blow, to blast
脸	臉	liǎn	n.	face
变化	變化	biànhuà	v.	to change
短袖		duǎnxiù	n.	short sleeve
短裤	短褲	duǎnkù	n.	shorts
夏天		xiàtiān	n.	summer
冬天		dōngtiān	n.	winter
只有		zhǐyǒu	adj.	only

A: 外头下着雪呢，还不到20度。风刮到脸上真不舒服。

B: 这儿的天气变化得很快。昨天还像夏天，有人穿短袖衬衫和短裤，今天就下起雪来了。这儿的夏天热，冬天冷，只有春天秋天比较舒服。不过，四五月常常下雨。出去的时候，得带雨伞，很不方便。

春天		chūntiān	n.	spring
秋天		qiūtiān	n.	fall
不过	不過	búguò	adv.	however
四月		sìyuè	n.	April
五月		wǔyuè	n.	May
下雨		xiàyǔ	v.o.	to rain
带	帶	dài	v.	to bring
雨伞	雨傘	yǔsǎn	n.	umbrella
方便		fāngbiàn	adj.	convenient

A: Wǒ juéde xiàyǔ bǐ xiàxuě hǎo.Xiàxuě de shíhou, kāichē zǒulù dōu hěn wēixiǎn, yíbùxiǎoxīn, jiù huì chūshìr.

B: Kěshì xiàxuě de shíhou hěn piàoliang, shùshang, lùshang, fángzi shang, dàochù dōu shì báisè de. Hǎokàn jíle!

A: Kāichē de shíhou, hǎokàn bù hǎokàn méi shénme guānxi, zhòngyào de shì ānquán bù ānquán. Yīnwèi wǒ děi kāichē, suǒyǐ wǒ zuì pà xiàxuě. Yí xiàxuě, wǒ jiù kěndìng huì chídào.

B: Wǒ zhù zài sùshè lǐ jiù méiyǒu zhèigè wèntí. Wúlùn xiàyǔ háishì xiàxuě, wǒ dōu búhuì chídào.

A: I think raining is better than snowing. When it snows, walking and driving are both dangerous. As soon as you become careless, you'll have an accident.

B: But it's beautiful when it's snowing. It's white everywhere: on the trees, in the streets, and on the houses. It's extremely pretty!

A: When you drive, whether it is pretty or not doesn't matter. The important thing is whether or not it's safe. Because I have to drive, I'm most afraid of snowing. Once it snows, I surely will be late.

B: I live in the dorm, so I don't have that problem. No matter if it rains or snows, I won't be late.

A: 我觉得下雨比下雪好。下雪的时候，开车走路都很危险，一不小心，就会出事儿。

B: 可是下雪的时候很漂亮，树上、路上、房子上，到处都是白色的。好看极了！

A: 开车的时候，好看不好看没什么关系，重要的是安全不安全。因为我得开车，所以我最怕下雪。一下雪，我就肯定会迟到。

B: 我住在宿舍里就没有这个问题，无论下雨还是下雪，我都不会迟到。

开车	開車	kāichē	v.o.	to drive a car
危险	危險	wēixiǎn	adj.	dangerous
一……就……		yī … jiù …	conj.	once … , then … ; as soon as … , then
出事(儿)	出事(兒)	chūshì	v.o	to have an accident
树	樹	shù	n.	tree
房子		fángzi	n.	house
到处	到處	dàochù	adv.	everywhere
没关系	沒關係	méiguānxì	phrase	doesn't matter
安全		ānquán	adj.	safe, secure
无论……都	無論……都	wúlùn … dōu	conj.	no matter

语法 Grammar Notes

1. Clothes and the Measure Word 件

In the text, a few terms for clothes are introduced: 衬衫 (shirt), 短袖衬衫 (short-sleeve shirt), 毛衣 (sweater), 大衣 (overcoat), and 短裤 (shorts). While the measure word 件 can be used for the first four, another measure word 条, which we'll learn in the next lesson, should be used for 短裤.

> ▶ 你怎么只穿一件衬衫啊？
>
> How come you're only wearing a shirt？
>
> 妈妈给我买了一件大衣。
>
> Mother bought me an overcoat.

2. 怕 (to fear, to be afraid) vs. 恐怕 (I'm afraid that ...)

怕 is a verb and can take nouns, verb phrases, and clauses as its objects. Like other emotion verbs, it can be modified by adverbs of degree, such as 很, 非常, 最, 极了, etc.

> 晚上一个人走路，你怕不怕？
>
> Are you afraid of walking alone at night?

恐怕 is an adverb. Do not use it to describe physical fear. It is about future possibility and carries the mild sense of worry or light concern in the tone of the speaker.

> ▶ 你这样出去，恐怕会感冒。
>
> If you go out like this, I'm afraid you'll catch a cold
>
> 恐怕他又要迟到了。 I am afraid that he will be late again.
> 他恐怕又要迟到了。

The two sentences above are identical in meaning. The subject of 恐怕 is always an understood 我, and not the subject of the main sentence. This is true whether 恐怕 appears before or after the subject.

3. 挺 + Adj./Emotion Verb 的

It is a colloquial expression, meaning rather, quite.

> ▶ 教室里挺暖和的。
>
> It was pretty warm in the classroom.
>
> 北京的冬天挺冷的。
>
> In Beijing, it is rather cold in winter.

我挺喜欢吃牛排的。

I quite like to eat the steak.

4. 到处都有/是 Object

到处都有/是 is used to emphasize the prevalence of something. If you want to specify the location, the place word can be put before 到处都有/是。

▶ 下雪的时候，到处都是白色的。
When it snows, it's white everywhere.

屋子里到处都是你的书。 or
你的书屋子里到处都是。
Your books are everywhere in the room.

Note in the two sentences above, despite the different locations of the object, that is, 你的书, the meaning of the sentence remains the same. Therefore, the following two structures are interchangeable.

到处都是/有 object

Object 到处都是/有

5. Describing the Weather

(1) Months and seasons

The twelve months in Chinese are easy to remember: count from one to twelve with 月 added to the number: 一月, 二月, 三月 up to 十二月. The four seasons in Chinese are: 春天, 夏天, 秋天, 冬天.

▶ 昨天还像夏天。　　　　It was still like summer yesterday.
这儿的夏天热，冬天冷。　It's hot in summer and cold in winter here.
春天天气真好。　　　　Spring weather is really nice.

(2) Temperature

The adjectives 冷 (cold), 热 (hot), 暖和 (warm), and 凉快 (liángkuài, cool) are used to describe the temperature. A degree of temperature is 度。

(3) Weather terms without subjects

Most weather terms in Chinese are verb-object expressions without subjects, including 下雨 (it rains), 下雪 (it snows), 刮风 (it's windy).

▶ 今天就下起雪来了。　　Today it started to snow (suddenly).
四五月常常下雨。　　　It often rains in April and May.

6. 不到 + Amount (less, fewer than)

Meaning less than, or not reaching a certain amount or number, 不到 is usually followed by a number denoting a small quantity or a brief period of time. It's often used with 就 to indicate less or fewer than the speaker's expectation.

▶ 还不到20度。
It is not even 20 degrees yet.

还不到6点他就起来了。
He got up when it was not even six o'clock yet.

7. V.P. + 的时候 (when ...)

▶ 出去的时候，穿上大衣，就没有问题了。
There won't be a problem if I put on my overcoat when going out.

下雪的时候，开车走路都很危险。
When it snows, walking and driving are both dangerous.

8. 不过 (however)

▶ 只有春天秋天比较舒服。不过，四五月常下雨。
Only in spring and fall is it relatively comfortable; however, it often rains in April and May.

有车很方便，不过，下雪的时候开车不安全。
It is convenient to have a car; however, it is not safe to drive when it snows.

9. 一……就…… (as soon as ... then ... ; once ... then ...)

▶ 一不小心，就会出事儿。
As soon as you become careless, you'll have an accident.

一下雪，我就肯定迟到。
Once it snows, I'll be late for sure.

我一吃西瓜，就觉得不舒服。
As soon as I eat watermelon, I feel uncomfortable.

10. ……没有(什么)关系，重要的是…… (... doesn't matter, the important thing is ...)

This sentence pattern points out the more important aspect of a matter in comparison to other aspects. "V. not V." is often used to structure the topics used in the positions of subject and object.

▶ 开车的时候，好看不好看没什么关系，重要的是安全不安全。

When you drive, whether it is pretty or not doesn't matter. The important thing is whether or not it's safe.

我的朋友买鞋的时候，样子和颜色对他都没有什么关系，重要的是舒服不舒服。

When my friend buys shoes, both the style and color don't matter to him. The important thing is whether or not they are comfortable.

11. 无论……都 (no matter ... ; regardless of ...)

无论……都 must be followed by one of three question forms:

无论 + question word + (subject) 都

无论 + V. 不 V. + (subject) 都 (this also applies to adjectives)

无论 + A 还是 B + (subject) 都

▶ 无论下雨还是下雪，我都不会迟到。

No matter if it rains or snows, I won't be late.

无论春夏秋冬，他都只穿一件衬衫。

No matter whether it is spring, summer, fall, or winter, he only wears a shirt.

(Note: Although this sentence does not explicitly include one of the three question forms listed above, in this situation the selective question "还是" is implied when the seasons are listed.)

The sentence can also be written as:

无论是不是夏天，他都只穿一件短袖衬衫。

Regardless of whether it's summer or not, he only wears a shirt.

无论是夏天还是冬天，他都只穿一件衬衫。

It doesn't matter if it's summer or winter, he only wears a shirt.

Cultural Notes

Measurements in China

Chinese measurements went through many different changes and developments throughout history. The most famous and influential episode in this long process was when the First Emperor (259 BCE–210 BCE) of the Qin Dynasty enforced uniformity in currency and measures throughout the empire after he unified China in 221 BCE. At the beginning of the twentieth century, international standards were introduced to China and adopted by governments at the time.

Coinage used by the other six states and the unification of the monetary system under the Qin Dynasty (left-hand image © Aketkov/Dreamstime.com; right-hand image © Bigchen/Dreamstime.com).

Measures for weight and volume in the Qin Dynasty (221 BCE–206 BCE) (weight from Henan Museum, China; bowl © SACU.org).

The current system of units of measurements used in China was restandardized and enforced throughout the country in the 1980s. It follows the metric system, with the addition of some traditional Chinese measures. The system of measurements in the United States is different from the metric system; therefore, when Chinese people first come to the United States or vice versa, they need to convert measurements between the two systems.

In this lesson, we learned how to express temperature in Chinese. In China, 摄氏 (shèshì, Celsius or centigrade) is used instead of 华氏 (huáshì, Fahrenheit). 冰点 (bīngdiǎn, freezing point) is zero degrees centigrade, or 32 degrees Fahrenheit. 零下 (língxià, below zero) is often added before a number to express temperatures below the freezing point. For example, 零下20度 (língxià 20 dù, 20 degree below the freezing point).

Some of the most often used units in the two countries are listed in the following table for your reference.

美国	中国	Conversion
磅 (bàng, pound)	斤 (jīn, half kilogram)	1 斤 = 1.1 磅
英尺 (yīngchǐ, feet)	米 (mǐ, meter)	1 米 = 3.3 英尺
英里 (yīnglǐ, mile)	公里 (gōnglǐ, kilometer)	1 公里 = 0.62 英里
华氏度 (Fahrenheit)	摄氏度 (Celsius)	32°F = 0°C

Traditional Character Text

下雪了

（A——張三，B——丁一）

A: 今天這麼冷，你怎麼只穿一件襯衫啊？

B: 天氣冷是冷，可是教室里挺暖和的，穿上毛衣就不舒服了。

A: 你這樣出去，恐怕會感冒。

B: 出去的時候，穿上大衣，就沒有問題了。

A: 外頭下着雪呢，還不到20度，風刮到臉上真不舒服。

B: 這兒的天氣變化得很快。昨天還像夏天，有人穿短袖襯衫和短褲，今天就下起雪來了。這兒的夏天熱，冬天冷，只有春天秋天比較舒服。不過，四五月常常下雨。出去的時候，得帶雨傘，很不方便。

A: 我覺得下雨比下雪好。下雪的時候，開車走路都很危險，一不小心，就會出事兒。

B: 可是下雪的時候很漂亮，樹上、路上、房子上，到處都是白色的。好看極了！

A: 開車的時候，好看不好看沒什麼關係，重要的是安全不安全。因為我得開車，所以我最怕下雪。一下雪，我就肯定會遲到。

B: 我住在宿舍里就沒有這個問題，無論下雨還是下雪，我都不會遲到。

16 Yuèláiyuèpàng, Zěnme Bàn?
(Getting Fatter, What Shall I Do?)

Pinyin Text

(A—Xiǎoyīng, B—Māma)

A: Mā, wǒ shàng dàxué yǐhòu, pàngle shí jǐ bàng. Zěnme cáinéng shòudiǎnr?

B: Nǐ cóngxiǎo jiù xǐhuān chīròu, bù xǐhuān chī qīngcài. Nǐ bùnéng zhǐ chīròu, bù chī qīngcài a.

A: Niúròu zhūròu wǒ zǎojiù bù chī le. Xiànzài wǒ měitiān zhǐ chī shēngcài, kěshì háishì yuèláiyuèpàng, wǒ bù zhīdào gāi zěnme bàn.

B: Zài jiā de shíhou, nǐ xǐhuān chī tiándiǎn, xiànzài shìbúshì hái měitiān dōu chī bīngqílín a?

A: Wǒ zuì xǐhuān qiǎokelì bīngqílín, wǎnfàn yǐhòu, zǒngyào chī yì diǎnr.

English Translation

(A—Xiaoying, B—Mother)

A: Mom, after I got to college, I gained more than ten pounds. How can I get a little thinner?

B: You have liked meat and disliked green vegetables since you were a child. You cannot just eat meat without eating vegetables.

A: I stopped eating beef and pork a long time ago. Now, I eat just lettuce every day, but I'm still getting fatter. I don't know what I should do.

B: When you were home, you liked dessert. Do you still eat ice cream every day?

A: Chocolate ice cream is my favorite. I always have a little bit after dinner.

第十六课 越来越胖，怎么办？

（A——小英，B——妈妈）

A：妈，我上大学以后，胖了十几磅。怎么才能瘦点儿？

B：你从小就喜欢吃肉，不喜欢吃青菜。你不能只吃肉，不吃青菜啊。

A：牛肉猪肉我早就不吃了。现在，我每天只吃生菜，可是还是越来越胖，我不知道该怎么办。

B：在家的时候，你喜欢吃甜点，现在是不是还每天都吃冰淇淋啊？

A：我最喜欢巧克力冰淇淋，晚饭以后，总要吃一点儿。

怎么办		zěnmebàn	phrase	what to do/how to deal with the situation
大学	大學	dàxué	n.	college, university
磅		bàng	n.	pound
瘦		shòu	adj.	skinny
从小	從小	cóngxiǎo	phrase	from a young age, since childhood
青菜		qīngcài	n.	green vegetables
牛肉		niúròu	n.	beef
猪肉		zhūròu	n.	pork
生菜		shēngcài	n.	lettuce
该	該	gāi	aux.v.	should, same as 应该
巧克力		qiǎokèlì	n.	chocolate

B：Wǒ kàn, nǐ búshì chī yìdiǎnr, shì chī yídàhé ba!

A: Mā, wǒ chúle chī bīngqílín, méiyǒu biéde huài xíguàn. Yàoshì lián bīngqílín dōu bùchī, wǒ zhēn yào èsǐle.

B: Nà zěnme hái huì yuèláiyuèpàng ne? Shì bú shì méi yùndòng a? Yàoshì xiǎng jiǎnféi nǐ děi shǎochī dōngxi duō yùndòng.

A: Zuòyè tàiduōle, méi shíjiān yùndòng.

B: Nǐ yǐqián měige xīngqī dōu dǎ yícì wǎngqiú. Xiànzài hái dǎbudǎ qiú ne?

A: Yǐjīng sāngè xīngqī méidǎle. Wǎngqiúchǎng lí sùshè tàiyuǎn le, tiānqì yòu bùhǎo, suǒyǐ hěncháng shíjiān méidǎ le. Qíshí, yuè yùndòng yuè è, yuè è jiù chīde yuèduō, chīde yuèduō jiù yuèpàng.

B: Nǐ yùndòng de hái búgòu, nǐ děi qù tǐyùguǎn pǎobù.

B: I think you don't just have a little bit, but a big box!

A: Mom, except eating ice cream, I don't have other bad habits. If I don't even eat ice cream, I'll starve to death.

B: Then how could you be getting fatter and fatter? Is it that you don't exercise? If you want to lose weight, you have to eat less and exercise more.

A: I have too much homework, and no time to exercise.

B: You used to play tennis once a week. Do you still play tennis now?

A: I haven't played for three weeks. The tennis court is too far away from my dorm, and besides, the weather isn't good, so I haven't played for a long time. In fact, the more you exercise, the hungrier you are; the hungrier you are, the more you eat; the more you eat, the fatter you get.

B: You didn't exercise enough. You need to do some running in the gym.

坏	壞	huài	adj.	bad
饿	餓	è	adj.	hungry
死		sǐ	v.	to die (adj. + 死了：extremely …)
运动	運動	yùndòng	v./n.	to do sports, sports

B：我看，你不是吃一点儿，是吃一大盒吧！

A：妈，我除了吃冰淇淋，没有别的坏习惯。要是连冰淇淋都不吃，我真要饿死了。

B：那怎么还会越来越胖呢？是不是没运动啊？要是想减肥，你 得少吃东西多运动。

A：作业太多了，没时间运动。

B：你以前每个星期都打一次网球，现在还打不打球呢？

A：已经三个星期没打了。网球场离宿舍太远了，天气又不好，所以很长时间没打了。其实，越运动越饿，越饿就吃得越多，吃得越多就越胖。

B：你运动得还不够，你得去体育馆跑步。

减肥	减肥	jiǎnféi	v.	to lose weight
时间		shíjiān	n.	time
以前		yǐqián	prep./t.w.	before … , … ago; in the past
网球	網球	wǎngqiú	n.	tennis
打球		dǎqiú	v.o.	to play ball games
网球场	網球場	wǎngqiúchǎng	n.	tennis court
离		lí	prep.	from
远	遠	yuǎn	adj.	far
够	夠	gòu	adj./adv.	enough
体育馆	體育館	tǐyùguǎn	n.	gym
长	長	cháng	adj.	long
跑步		pǎobù	v.o.	to run, to jog

A: Wǒ zhīdào, kěshì shuōqǐlái róngyì, zuòqǐlái nán a! Wǒ pàng le shí jǐ bàng, yīfu kùzi dōu xiǎole, chuānzhe hěn bù shūfu, děi mǎi xīn yīfu le.

B: Nèitiáo niúzǎikù shì nǐ qù xuéxiào yǐqián mǎi de, xiànzài hái chuān de xià ma?

A: Gēnběn chuān búxiàle. Kùzi hǎoxiàng biàn xiǎo le, yě biàn duǎn le.

B: Búshi kùzi biàn xiǎo le, shì nǐ biàn pàng le.

A: I know, but that's easier said than done. I have gained more than ten pounds. My clothes and pants all got smaller and very uncomfortable. I have to buy some new clothes.

B: That pair of jeans was just bought before you went to college. Do they still fit?

A: I cannot wear them at all. My pants seem to have become smaller and shorter.

B: It's not that the pants became smaller, but that you became fatter.

衣服	yīfu	n.	clothes
裤子	kùzi	n.	pants
新	xīn	adj.	new
条	tiáo	n.	measure word for pants (and things with a long and lean shape)

A：我知道，可是说起来容易，做起来难啊！我胖了十几磅，衣服裤子都小了，穿着很不舒服，得买新衣服了。

B：那条牛仔裤是你去学校以前买的，现在还穿得下吗？

A：根本穿不下了。裤子好像变小了，也变短了。

B：不是裤子变小了，是你变胖了。

牛仔裤	牛仔褲	niúzǎikù	n.	jeans
学校	學校	xuéxiào	n.	school
变	變	biàn	v.	to become, to change
短		duǎn	adj.	short

语法 Grammar Notes

1. 早就……了 (something happened a long time ago)

▶ 猪肉牛肉我早就不吃了！

I gave up eating pork and beef a long time ago.

她早就结婚了！

She married a long time ago.

2. Review

越来越 + adj./emotion verb   more and more

越……越……   the more … , the more …

越来越…… functions as an adverb indicating the increasing intensity in degree of the adjective or emotion verb following it.

▶ 我每天只吃生菜，可是还是越来越胖。

I eat only lettuce every day, but I'm still getting fatter and fatter.

天气越来越冷。

It is getting colder and colder.

越……越…… indicates that a second state of affairs advances along with its preceding state. The subjects in the two clauses can be either the same or different.

Subj. 1 越 + verb phrase/adj., (subj. 2) 越 + verb phrase/adj.

▶ 越运动越饿，越饿就吃得越多，吃得越多就越胖。

The more you exercise, the hungrier you are; the hungrier you are, the more you eat; the more you eat, the fatter you become.

我越喝水越觉得饿。

The more water I drink, the hungrier I feel.

妈妈越不让我吃甜点，我越想吃。

The more mother asks me not to have dessert, the more I want to eat.

3. 以前 (... ago, before ... ; in the past)

以前 may stand by itself as a time word, meaning "in the past."

▶ 你以前每个星期都打一次网球。

In the past, you used to play tennis once every week.

以前 can also be appended to a time word, an action, or an event to indicate a time before that referential point.

▶ 那条牛仔裤是你去学校以前买的。

That pair of jeans was bought before you went to college.

回家以前我给妈妈打了一个电话。

I called my mother before going home.

以前 can be appended to a time duration to indicate some time ago.

▶ 三个星期以前我就做完作业了。

I finished my homework three weeks ago.

4. Time Duration

Subject + V. + O. + (已经) V. + 了 ＋ time duration (了)

This pattern is to express time duration in an **affirmative sentence** in which a verb takes an object. The optional 了 at the end of the sentence indicates that the action is still in progress at the present and will possibly continue in the future. The words of time duration that we have learned so far are only 星期 (week) and 学期 (semester). Other common time duration words and their usages will be introduced in future lessons, such as 天 (tiān, day), 月 (yuè, month), and 年 (nián, year).

▶ 我打网球打了三个星期了。

I have been playing tennis for three weeks.

我学中文已经学了一个学期了。

I have been learning Chinese for a semester.

As for time duration in a **negative sentence**, the following pattern can be used:

Subject + (已经) time duration 没 V. (O.) 了

▶ 已经三个星期没打了。

I haven't played for three weeks.

我已经一个学期没给朋友打电话了。

I haven't called my friend for a semester.

To ask a question about time duration, one may use 多长时间 (how long):

你多长时间没打网球了？

How long have you not play tennis?

5. Frequency

每 + time duration + V. + number 次 (O.)

▶ 你以前每个星期都打一次网球。

You used to play tennis once a week.

我每个学期回两次家。

I go home twice every semester.

6. 又

In this text, 又 means on top of, in addition to, or moreover. It's often used to introduce a second reason.

▶ 网球场离宿舍太远了，天气又不好，所以很长时间没打了。

The tennis court is far away from my dorm, and besides, the weather isn't great, so I haven't played for a long time.

他吃得多，又不运动，所以越来越胖了。

He eats a lot, and in addition to that he doesn't exercise, so he is getting fatter.

7. 多／少 + V. (do more or less of something)

This pattern is often used in an imperative sentence to give suggestions.

▶ 要是想减肥，你得少吃东西多运动。

If you want to lose weight, you'll have to eat less and exercise more.

妈妈让孩子多吃青菜。

Mother asked the children to eat more vegetables.

8. 够 (adj./adv.) (enough)

(1) Something 够了。   … is enough.
Something 不够。   … is not enough.

▶ 你运动得还不够。

You didn't exercise enough.

我的钱不够。

I don't have enough money (literally, "My money is not enough").

Note that 够 is usually used not as a pre-noun modifier, but as a predicate. Therefore, for "enough money," it is WRONG to say "够的钱," but correct to say "钱够了."

(2) 够 can also be used as an adverb to modify an adjective. In English, "enough" is placed after the adjective, while in Chinese, 够 precedes the adjective.

你已经够胖了。   You are already fat enough.
我吃得够多了。   I have eaten enough.

9. V. 得下 / V. 不下 (to indicate capacity or ability to contain or hold)

我的宿舍太小，住不下四个人。

My dorm is too small for four people to live in it.

我们的教室坐得下一百个学生。

Our classroom is big enough for one hundred students to sit in it.

(衣服、裤子、鞋) 穿得下 means clothes, pants, shoes are still big enough to fit into. The negative form is 穿不下.

▶那条牛仔裤现在还穿得下吗？

Does that pair of jeans still fit?

上个学期买的衣服我现在已经穿不下了。

I already cannot fit into the clothes that I bought last semester.

Traditional Character Text

越來越胖，怎麼辦？

（A——小英，B——媽媽）

A：媽，我上大學以後，胖了十幾磅。怎麼才能瘦點儿？

B：你從小就喜歡吃肉，不喜歡吃青菜。你不能只吃肉，不吃青菜啊。

A：牛肉豬肉我早就不吃了。現在，我每天只吃生菜，可是還是越來越胖，
   我不知道該怎麼辦。

B：在家的時候，你喜歡吃甜點，現在是不是還每天都吃冰淇淋啊？

A：我最喜歡巧克力冰淇淋，晚飯以後，總要吃一點兒。

B：我看，你不是吃一點兒，是吃一大盒吧！

A：媽，我除了吃冰淇淋，沒有別的坏習慣。要是連冰淇淋都不吃，我真要餓死了。

B：那怎麼還會越來越胖呢？是不是沒運動啊？要是想減肥，你得少吃東西多運動。

A：作業太多了，沒時間運動。

B：你以前每個星期都打一次網球，現在還打不打球呢？

A：已經三個星期沒打了。網球場離宿舍太遠了，天氣又不好，所以很長時間沒打了。其實，越運動越餓，越餓吃得越多，吃得越多就越胖。

B： 你運動得還不夠，你得去體育館跑步。

A：我知道，可是説起來容易，做起來難啊！我胖了十幾磅，衣服褲子都小了，穿著很不舒服，得買新衣服了。

B：那條牛仔褲是你去學校以前買的，現在還穿得下嗎？

A：根本穿不下了。褲子好像變小了，也變短了。

B：不是褲子變小了，是你變胖了。

17 Qí Zìxíngchē
(Ride a Bike)

Pinyin Text

(A—Xiǎoyīng, B—Bàba)

A: Zhù zài xuéxiào lǐ, méi chē, zhēn bù fāngbiàn, dào nǎr dōu děi zǒulù. Nín néng-bunéng bāng wǒ mǎi liàng chē?

B: Xiàoyuán lǐ búshì yǒu xiàochē ma?

A: Yǒushiyǒu, kěshì děi děng, yǒushíhou yì děng jiùshi bàn ge xiǎoshí. Tài làngfèi shíjiān le.

B: Nǐmen xuéxiào bìngbúdà, nǐde sùshè lí jiàoshì yě bùyuǎn, zǒulù shíwǔ fēnzhōng jiù dàole ba. Érqiě tíngchē yěshì yíge dà wèntí. Yǒule chē huì gèng máfan de.

English Translation

(A—Xiaoying, B—Father)

A: It is really inconvenient to live on campus without a car. I have to walk everywhere. Could you help me buy a car?

B: Aren't there shuttles?

A: Although there are shuttles, I have to wait for them. Sometimes it takes half an hour. It's a waste of time.

B: Your school is actually not big, and your dorm is not far from the classrooms. It only takes fifteen minutes to walk there, right? Furthermore, parking is also a big problem. It will be even more troublesome to have a car.

骑	騎	qí	v.	to ride (bikes or horses, but not for cars, buses)
自行车	自行車	zìxíngchē	n.	bike
校园	校園	xiàoyuán	n.	campus
校车	校車	xiàochē	n.	campus shuttle
等		děng	v.	to wait

第十七课 骑自行车

（A——小英，B——爸爸）

A：住在学校里，没车，真不方便，到哪儿都得走路。您能不能帮我买辆车？

B：校园里不是有校车吗？

A：有是有，可是得等，有时候一等就是半个小时。太浪费时间了。

B：你们学校并不大，你的宿舍离教室也不远，走路15分钟就到了吧。而且停车也是一个大问题。有了车会更麻烦的。

有时候	有時候	yǒu shíhòu	t.w.	sometimes
小时	小時	xiǎoshí	n.	hour
浪费	浪費	làngfèi	v.	to waste
分钟	分鐘	fēnzhōng	n.	minute
停车	停車	tíngchē	v.o.	to stop the car; to park the car
更		gèng	adv.	even more

A: Wǒ bìng búshì yào kāichē qù shàngkè, zhōumò xiǎng qù fùjìn de chāoshì mǎi diǎnr dōngxi, méichē, gēnběn bù kěnéng.

B: Wèi shénme búzuò gōngjiāochē ne?

A: Gōngjiāochē tàishǎo le, yíge xiǎoshí cái yìbān.

B: Mǎi liàng chē tàiguìle, jiālǐ de qián búgòu.

A: Bà, nín búshì yǒu yíliàng jiùchē ma? Néngbunéng bǎ nèi liàng jiùchē gěiwǒ?

B: Nèi liàng jiùchē chángcháng chū wèntí, wǒ bú fàngxīn ràng nǐ kāi.

A: Xīnchē bùnéng mǎi, jiùchē bùnéng kāi, nà wǒ zěnme bàn a?

A: It is not that I want to drive to class. If I want to go to nearby grocery stores on the weekend, it is completely impossible without a car.

B: Why don't you take the bus?

A: There are too few buses. There is only one bus every hour.

B: It is too expensive to buy a car. Our family doesn't have enough money.

A: Dad, don't you have an old car? Can you give that old car to me?

B: That old car often has problems. I feel uncomfortable letting you drive it.

A: I can't buy a new car, and can't drive the old car, either. What should I do then?

A：我并不是要开车去上课，周末想去附近的超市买点儿东西，没车，根本不可能。

B：为什么不坐公交车呢？

A：公交车太少了，一个小时才一班。

B：买辆车太贵了，家里的钱不够。

A：爸，您不是有一辆旧车吗？能不能把那辆旧车给我？

B：那辆旧车常常出问题，我不放心让你开。

A：新车不能买，旧车不能开，那我怎么办啊？

周末		zhōumò	n.	weekend
附近		fùjìn	adj./n.	nearby
超市		chāoshì	n.	supermarket, grocery store
公交车	公交車	gōngjiāochē	n.	bus
才		cái	adv.	only
班		bān	m.w.	measure word for bus service
旧	舊	jiù	adj.	old, used
出问题	出問題	chū wèntí	v.o.	to have problems
放心		fàngxīn	v.o.	reassured, to set one's heart at rest

B: Yěxǔ kěyǐ mǎi yí liàng zìxíngchē, zài xiàoyuán lǐ qí zìxíngchē yòu fāngbiàn yòu ānquán.

A: Zhè zhēn shì ge hǎo zhúyì! Zuìjìn, yìtiāndàowǎn zuòzhe xuéxí, shénme yùndòng dōu méiyǒu, qí zìxíngchē duànliàn duànliàn tǐnghǎode. Mǎi zìxíngchē, wǒde qián kǒngpà búgòu.

B: Nà nǐ yòng xìnyòngkǎ mǎi ba.

A: Hǎo, wǒ míngtiān jiù qù mǎi.

B: Maybe you can buy a bike. Riding a bike on campus is both convenient and safe.

A: This is indeed a good idea. Recently, I have been sitting and studying day and night. I don't exercise at all. It would be quite good to ride a bike and get a workout. I'm afraid that I don't have enough money to buy a bike.

B: In that case you can buy it with your credit card.

A: Okay, I will go buy one tomorrow.

也许	也許	yěxǔ	adv.	perhaps, probably
可以		kěyǐ	aux.	may
主意		zhúyì	n.	idea
最近		zuìjìn	t.w.	recently
一天到晚		yìtiāndàowǎn	t.w.	from dawn to dusk
锻炼	鍛煉	duànliàn	v.	to exercise, to work out

B：也许可以买一辆自行车，在校园里骑自行车又方便又安全。

A：这真是个好主意！最近，一天到晚坐着学习，什么运动都没有，骑自行车锻炼锻炼挺好的。买自行车，我的钱恐怕不够。

B：那你用信用卡买吧。

A：好，我明天就去买。

语法 Grammar Notes

1. Review: Interrogative pronoun (哪儿, 谁, 什么)……都

This sentence pattern is used to describe a universal situation that has no exceptions: everywhere (wherever), everybody (whoever), everything (whatever), and so on. Interrogative pronouns can also combine with verbs or prepositions to become phrases, for example, 去哪儿, 在哪儿.

▶ 到哪儿都得走路。
Wherever I go, I have to walk.

美国的车很便宜, 谁都有车。
Cars are very cheap in the United States. Everybody has a car.

2. 一V. 就是 + Time Duration/Amount (once it starts, the action will last for …)

It most often carries a tone of excessiveness (a long time or large amount).

▶ 有时候一等就是半小时。
Sometimes [I have to] wait for half an hour.

这儿冬天虽然不常下雪, 可是一下就是一个星期。
Although it does not often snow here in the winter, once it snows, it will keep snowing for a week.

他很喜欢喝咖啡, 一喝就是很多杯。
He likes to drink coffee very much. Once he starts, he will drink many cups.

A variance of this pattern is to replace 是 with the specific verb:

一V. 就V. + time duration/amount

So the above examples can be rewritten as follows:

有时候一等就等半小时。
这儿冬天虽然不常常下雪, 可是一下就下一个星期。
他很喜欢喝咖啡, 一喝就喝很多杯。

3. 浪费 + Object (to waste (resources))

The objects that are most commonly used with 浪费 are resources, such as 水(water), 电 (electricity), 钱 (money), and 时间 (time).

▶ 太浪费时间了。　　　It's a huge waste of time.

别浪费水。　　　　Do not waste water.

4. Review: Subject 并不 adj./v.

并 "actually (not)" can precede only the negative adverbs 不 or 没(有). It negates a previous statement or assumption.

▶ 你们学校并不大，你的宿舍离教室也不远。

Your school is actually not big, your dorm is also not far from the classroom. (The second clause of "subj. 也不 adj./v." is added to provide additional information.)

▶ 我并不是要开车去上课。

It is not that I want to drive to class.

5. 更 + Adjective/Emotion Verb (even more)

▶ 有了车会更麻烦的。

It will be even more troublesome to have a car.

更 can be used in an explicit comparison sentence with 比:

A 比 B 更 adj./emotion verb

A is even more … than B

他的中文说得比你更好。

He speaks Chinese even better than you do.

6. Something 出问题 (there are problems with something/something goes wrong)

The subject is usually a thing, not a person.

他的电脑出问题了。

There was something wrong with his computer.

他今天走路来上课，因为他的自行车出问题了。

He walked to class today, because there was a problem with his bike.

Traditional Character Text

騎自行車

（A——小英，B——爸爸）

A：住在學校裏，沒車，真不方便，到哪兒都得走路。您能不能幫我買輛車？

B：校園裏不是有校車嗎？

A：有是有，可是得等，有時候一等就是半個小時。太浪費時間了。

B：你們學校並不大，你的宿舍離教室也不遠，走路15分鐘就到了吧，而且停車也是一個大問題。有了車會更麻煩的。

A：我並不是要開車去上課，週末想去附近的超市買點兒東西，沒車，根本不可能。

B：為什麼不坐公交車呢？

A：公交車太少了，一個小時才一班。

B：買輛車太貴了，家裏的錢不夠。

A：爸，您不是有一輛舊車嗎？能不能把那輛舊車給我？

B：那輛舊車常常出問題，我不放心讓你開。

A：新車不能買，舊車不能開，那我怎麼辦啊？

B：也許可以買一輛自行車，在校園裏騎自行車又方便又安全。

A：這真是個好主意！最近，一天到晚坐著學習，什麼運動都沒有，騎自行車鍛煉鍛煉挺好的。買自行車，我的錢恐怕不夠。

B：那你用信用卡買吧。

A：好，我明天就去買。

18

Zìxíngchē Bèi Tōule
(The Bike Was Stolen)

Pinyin Text

(A—Xiǎoyīng, B—Māma)

A: Mā, wǒde zìxíngchē bèi tōu le.

B: Chē mǎile hái búdào yíge xīngqī, zěnme jiù bèi tōu le ne? Shì shénme shíhou bèi tōu de?

A: Shì zuótiān bèi tōu de.

B: Shì zàinǎr bèi tōu de?

A: Shì zài sùshè wàitou bèi tōu de.

B: Shì shéi tōu de a?

A: Jǐngchá shuō, kěnéng shì zhùzài fùjìn de háizi tōu de.

B: Shì zěnme tōu de a?

A: Xiǎotōu bǎ suǒ jiǎnduàn le.

English Translation

(A—Xiaoying, B—Mother)

A: Mom, my bike was stolen.

B: It's been less than a week since it was bought. How could it be stolen? When was it stolen?

A: It was stolen yesterday.

B: Where was it stolen?

A: It was stolen outside of the dorm.

B: Who did it?

A: The policeman said it probably was some kid from the neighborhood who stole the bike.

B: How was it stolen?

A: The thief cut the lock off the bike.

偷		tōu	v.	to steal
警察		jǐngchá	n.	police, policeman
小偷		xiǎotōu	n.	thief
锁	鎖	suǒ	n./v.	lock; to lock
剪		jiǎn	v.	to cut with scissors
断	斷	duàn	adj.	broken

第十八课 自行车被偷了

（A—小英，B—妈妈）

A：妈，我的自行车被偷了。

B：车买了还不到一个星期，怎么就被偷了呢？是什么时候被偷的？

A：是昨天被偷的。

B：是在哪儿被偷的？

A：是在宿舍外头被偷的。

B：是谁偷的啊？

A：警察说，可能是住在附近的孩子偷的。

B：是怎么偷的啊？

A：小偷把锁剪断了。

B: Zìxíngchē hái zhǎo de huílái ma?

A: Jǐngchá shuō, kěnéng zhǎo bu huílái le.

B: Wǒ yǐwéi xiàoyuán lǐ hěn ānquán, búhuì yǒu zhèyàng de shì.

A: Qíshí, cháng yǒu tóngxué diū dōngxi. Shàngge xīngqī, wǒ tóngwū de bǐjìběn diànnǎo diūle. Yǐjīng yíge xīngqī le, hái méi zhǎozháo ne.

B: Hǎozài nǐ diū de shì zìxíngchē, búshì diànnǎo, yàobùrán jiù gèng máfan le. Jìrán xuéxiào lǐ bù ānquán, nǐ jiù děi xiǎoxīn, chūqu de shíhou, bié wàngle suǒmén.

A: Hǎo, zhīdào le.

B: Can you still get the bike back?

A: The policeman said it was not very likely to get it back.

B: I thought the campus was safe and this sort of thing would not happen.

A: In fact, there are often students whose things get lost. Last week, my roommate lost her laptop. It has already been a week and the laptop still has not been found.

B: Fortunately what you lost was a bike. If it were a computer, it would be even more troublesome. Since it's not safe in school, you need to be careful. When you go out, don't forget to lock the door.

A: All right, I know.

同屋		tóngwū	n.	roommate
笔记本	筆記本	bǐjìběn	n.	notebook
笔记本电脑	筆記本電腦	bǐjìběn diànnǎo	n.	laptop
好在		hǎozài	adv.	fortunately

B：自行车还找得回来吗？

A：警察说，可能找不回来了。

B：我以为校园里很安全，不会有这样的事。

A：其实，常有同学丢东西。上个星期，我同屋的笔记本电脑丢了。已经一个星期了，还没找着呢。

B：好在你丢的是自行车，不是电脑，要不然就更麻烦了。既然学校里不安全，你就得小心，出去的时候，别忘了锁门。

A：好，知道了。

要不然	yàobùrán	conj.	otherwise
既然	jìrán	conj.	since, given the fact that …
忘了	wàngle	v.	to forget

语法 Grammar Notes

1. Review 被

被 is a passive voice marker. The passive voice is usually expressed in the following pattern:

Receiver of action + 被 + **doer of action** + **other elements**

我的车被弟弟开走了。

My car was driven away by my younger brother.

When the doer of the action is unknown, it can be omitted.

▶ 我的自行车被偷了。

My bike was stolen.

2. Review: 是⋯⋯的

This sentence pattern is used to report a past action or event with specific emphasis on its time, place, manner, or other circumstantial aspects related to the action.

Subject + 是 + **emphatic part** + **verb** + 的 + **object** (for V.O. construction)

Subject + 是 + **emphatic part** + **verb** + **object** + 的

▶ 你的自行车是什么时候被偷的？

When was your bike stolen?

When the subject is emphasized, 是 should be put before the subject.

▶ 是谁偷的？

Who stole it?

▶ 是住在附近的孩子偷的。

It was some kid from the neighborhood who stole (the bike).

3. 回来

"回来" can be used as a verb, meaning "to come back."

妈妈让我早点儿回来。
Mother asked me to come back earlier.

In "找回来," 回来 is used as a complement meaning "back."

找得回来	can get back	positive potential form
找不回来	cannot get back	negative potential form
找回来了	got back	positive resultative form
没找回来	didn't get back	negative resultative form

▶ 自行车还找得回来吗？
Can you still get the bike back?

4. 好在……，要不然…… (fortunately ... otherwise ...)

This pattern indicates that something fortunate has happened, otherwise a worse-case scenario would be expected.

▶ 好在你丢的是自行车，不是电脑，要不然就更麻烦了。
Fortunately, what you lost was a bike, not a computer. Otherwise, it would be even more troublesome.

我上课的时候睡着了。好在老师没看到，要不然她会很不高兴。
I fell asleep in class. Fortunately the teacher didn't see me. Otherwise, she would have been very unhappy.

5. 既然……就…… (since ... , then ... ; given the fact that ... , then ...)

▶ 既然学校里不安全，你就得小心。
Since it is not safe on campus, you should be careful.

既然你感冒了，就早点儿睡觉吧。
Since you have a cold, why not go to bed earlier?

Traditional Character Text

自行車被偷了

（A——小英，B——媽媽）

A：媽，我的自行車被偷了。

B：車買了還不到一個星期，怎麼就被偷了呢？是什麼時候被偷的？

A：是昨天被偷的。

B：是在哪兒被偷的？

A：是在宿舍外頭被偷的。

B：是誰偷的啊？

A：警察説，可能是住在附近的孩子偷的。

B：是怎麼偷的啊？

A：小偷把鎖剪斷了。

B：自行車還找得回來嗎？

A：警察説，可能找不回來了。

B：我以為校園裏很安全，不會有這樣的事。

A：其實，常有同學丟東西。上個星期，我同屋的筆記本電腦丟了。已經一個星期了，還沒找著呢。

B：好在你丟的是自行車，不是電腦，要不然就更麻煩了。既然學校裏不安全，你就得小心，出去的時候，別忘了鎖門。

A：好，知道了。

19 Zhōngguó Chéng (Chinatown)

Pinyin Text

(A—Zhāng Sān, B—Xiǎo Dīng)

A: Xiǎo Dīng, shàngge zhōumò nǐ dào nǎr qù le?

B: Wǒ hé tóngwū qùle yícì Niǔyuē de Zhōngguó chéng.

A: Nǐmen shì zěnme qù de? Shì zuò qìchē qù de, háishì zuò huǒchē qù de?

B: Wǒmen shì zuò huǒchē qù de.

A: Wèishénme búzuò gōnggòng qìchē ne?

B: Yīnwèi lùshang chángcháng dǔchē, kěshì huǒchē méiyǒu zhèige wèntí, érqiě huǒchē bǐ qìchē kuài.

A: Kěshì huǒchē bìng búdào Zhōngguó chéng a.

B: Dàole Niǔyuē de huǒchē zhàn, zhuǎn yícì dìtiě jiùdào Zhōngguó chéng le. Tǐng fāngbiàn de.

A: Nǐ zài Zhōngguó chéng shuō Zhōngguó huà le ma?

English Translation

(A—Zhang San, B—Xiao Ding)

A: Xiao Ding, where did you go last weekend?

B: I went to New York's Chinatown with my roommate.

A: How did you go? Did you go by bus or by train?

B: We went by train.

A: Why didn't you take the bus?

B: Because there are often traffic jams on the road, but the train doesn't have this problem. Furthermore, the train is faster than the bus.

A: However, the train does not go to Chinatown.

B: After arriving at the train station in New York, it only takes one transfer at the subway to get to Chinatown. It is quite convenient.

A: Did you speak Chinese in Chinatown?

| 城 | | chéng | n. | city, town |
| 中国城 | 中國城 | Zhōngguó chéng | n. | Chinatown |

第十九课 中国城

（A——张三，B——小丁）

A：小丁，上个周末你到哪儿去了？

B：我和同屋去了一次纽约的中国城。

A：你们是怎么去的？是坐汽车去的，还是坐火车去的？

B：我们是坐火车去的。

A：为什么不坐公共汽车呢？

B：因为路上常常堵车，可是火车没有这个问题，而且火车比汽车快。

A：可是火车并不到中国城啊。

B：到了纽约的火车站，转一次地铁就到中国城了，挺方便的。

A：你在中国城说中国话了吗？

汽车	汽車	qìchē	n.	bus, car
火车	火車	huǒchē	n.	train
公共汽车	公共汽車	gōnggòng qìchē	n.	(public) bus
堵车	堵車	dǔchē	n./v.	traffic jam; to have a traffic jam
站		zhàn	n.	station, stop
转	轉	zhuǎn	v.	to transfer
地铁	地鐵	dìtiě	n.	subway

B: Wǒmen qù le yìjiā Zhōngguó fànguǎnr. Wǒ gēn fúwùyuán shuō Pǔtōnghuà, dànshì fúwùyuán gēn wǒ shuō Yīngwén. Kāishǐ wǒ yǐwéi tā tīngbudǒng wǒde Zhōngwén, ràng wǒ tǐng shīwàng de; hòulái wǒ cái zhīdào, hěnduō fànguǎnr de fúwùyuán zhǐ huì shuō Guǎngdōng huà, búhuì shuō Pǔtōnghuà. Dàole Niǔyuē de Zhōngguó chéng, wǒ cái zhīdào, "Pǔtōnghuà" bìngbù "pǔtōng."

A: Nǐ xǐhuān nèijiā fànguǎnr de cài ma?

B: Wǒ diǎn le yíge jīròu, yǒudiǎnr là. Wǒde tóngwū diǎnle yìtiáoyú, shì dàitóu de, kànqǐlái yǒudiǎnr qíguài, kěshì chīqǐlái hǎochī jíle.

A: Zhōngguó cài dōu shì là de ma?

B: We went to a Chinese restaurant. I spoke Mandarin with the waitress, but the waitress spoke English with me. In the beginning, I thought she didn't understand my Chinese, which made me quite disappointed. Only later did I find out that many waiters in the restaurants only speak Cantonese and cannot speak Mandarin. Only after I got to New York's Chinatown did I know that the "Common Language" is actually not "common."

A: Did you like the dishes of that restaurant?

B: I ordered a chicken dish. It was a little spicy. My roommate ordered a fish which still had its head on. It looked a little strange, but it tasted very good.

A: Are all Chinese dishes spicy?

普通话	普通話	Pǔtōnghuà	n.	Mandarin, literally "common language"
但是		dànshì	conj.	but, similar to 可是
开始	開始	kāishǐ	n.	beginning; in the beginning
失望		shīwàng	adj.	disappointed
后来	後來	hòulái	t.w.	later

B：我们去了一家中国饭馆儿。我跟服务员说普通话，但是服务员跟我说英文。开始我以为他听不懂我的中文，让我挺失望的；后来我才知道，很多饭馆儿的服务员只会说广东话，不会说普通话。到了纽约的中国城，我才知道，"普通话"并不"普通"。

A：你喜欢那家饭馆儿的菜吗？

B：我点了一个鸡肉，有点儿辣。我的同屋点了一条鱼，是带头的，看起来有点儿奇怪，可是吃起来好吃极了。

A：中国菜都是辣的吗？

广东	廣東	Guǎngdōng	n.	Guangdong, Canton
广东话	廣東話	Guǎngdōng huà	n.	Cantonese
普通		pǔtōng	adj.	ordinary, common
点	點	diǎn	v.	to order (food)
鸡肉	雞肉	jīròu	n.	chicken meat
辣		là	adj.	spicy
带头	帶頭	dàitóu	v.o.	with the head on
奇怪		qíguài	adj.	strange

B: Búshì. Yǒude là, yǒude búlà. Zhōngguó cài, suān tián kǔ là, gèzhǒng wèidao dōu yǒu. Shànghǎi cài méiyǒu Běijīng cài nàme xián. Shànghǎi rén zuòcài de shíhou, yán fàngde bùduō, xǐhuān fàng cù hé táng, suǒyǐ Shànghǎi cài yòusuānyòutián.

A: Zhōngguó cài nǐ chīdeguàn chībúguàn?

B: Zhōngguó cài chīdeguàn, kěshì kuàizi yòngbúguàn. Wǒ háishì bǐjiào xíguàn yòng dāochā.

A: Xiàcì nǐ qù Zhōngguó chéng de shíhou, gěi wǒ dǎ ge diànhuà, wǒ yě qù.

B: Méi wèntí.

B: No. Some are spicy, some are not. Chinese food has all kinds of flavors: sour, sweet, bitter, and spicy. Shanghai dishes are not as salty as Beijing dishes. When Shanghainese cook, they don't put much salt in the dishes, but like to add vinegar and sugar; therefore, Shanghai dishes are both sour and sweet.

A: Are you able to get used to eating Chinese dishes?

B: I am able to get used to eating Chinese dishes, but I am not able to get used to using chopsticks. I am still more used to using knife and fork.

A: Next time when you go to Chinatown, give me a call. I will also go.

B: No problem.

酸	suān	adj.	sour
苦	kǔ	adj.	bitter
各种	gèzhǒng	phrase	all kinds of …
味道	wèidào	n.	flavor
咸	xián	adj.	salty
做菜	zuòcài	v.o.	to make dishes, to cook
盐	yán	n.	salt
醋	cù	n.	vinegar
糖	táng	n.	sugar
v.得/不惯……得/不惯……	de/búguàn	v.c.	able/unable to get used to doing …
习惯　　　　習慣	xíguàn	v.	be used to …

B：不是，有的辣，有的不辣。中国菜，酸甜苦辣，各种味道都
　　有。上海菜没有北京菜那么咸。上海人做菜的时候，盐放得
　　不多，喜欢放醋和糖，所以上海菜又酸又甜。

A：中国菜你吃得惯吃不惯？

B：中国菜吃得惯，可是筷子用不惯。我还是比较习惯用刀叉。

A：下次你去中国城的时候，给我打个电话，我也去。

B：没问题。

SeanPavonePhoto/Shutterstock.com

语法 Grammar Notes

1. Review: 是……的

When one talks about past events and wants to emphasize when, where, why, or how or the subject of the action that occurred, one should use this 是……的 structure. Elements that are to be emphasized should be put between 是 and 的.

For a regular sentence "I went to Chinatown by train with my roommate last weekend,"

(1) If the manner of the event, that is, "by train," is to be emphasized:

上个周末我和同屋是坐火车去的中国城。

It was by train that my roommate and I went to Chinatown last weekend.

(2) If the time of the event, that is, "last weekend," is to be emphasized:

我和同屋是上个周末去的中国城。

It was last weekend that my roommate and I went to Chinatown.

(3) If "with whom" is to be emphasized:

我是和我的同屋上个周末去的中国城。

It was with my roommate that I went to Chinatown last weekend.

2. Review: 并不/没(有) (actually not …)

Adverb 并 "actually" can only be followed by negative words 不 or 没/没有. It indicates that the fact is different from one's assumption.

▶ 火车并不到中国城。

The train actually doesn't go to Chinatown.

我并没有去过纽约的中国城。

I actually have not been to New York's Chinatown.

并 can be combined with 其实 qíshí, which also means "in fact, actually," to make the sentence more emphatic, but it does not have to.

"普通话"其实并不"普通"。

The "Common Language" (Mandarin) is actually not common.

3. 开始……, 后来…… (in the beginning ... , later ...)

This structure often indicates a change from the earlier situation. A derivative structure from this is:

开始以为……, 后来才知道……

In the beginning the speaker thought, not until later did he/she find out that ...

This structure indicates the correction of a mistaken opinion.

▶ 开始我以为他听不懂我的中文, 后来我才知道, 很多饭馆儿的服务员只会说广东话。

In the beginning, I thought he didn't understand my Chinese. Only later did I find out that many waiters in the restaurants only speak Cantonese.

开始我走路去上课, 后来我骑自行车去上课。

In the beginning I walked to class; later I rode my bike to class.

4. 失望 (disappointed)

A对B失望   A is disappointed in B
B让A失望   B made A disappointed

▶ 开始我以为他听不懂我的中文, 让我挺失望的。

In the beginning, I thought he couldn't understand my Chinese, which made me quite disappointed.

上大学、工作他都不喜欢。他的爸爸妈妈对他很失望。

He doesn't like to go to college or to work. His parents are very disappointed in him.

5. A, B, C ... , 各种 + noun (all kinds of ... , such as A, B, C ...)

The noun after 各种 is a general category and A, B, C are specific examples listed to represent the entire range.

▶ 中国菜, 酸甜苦辣, 各种味道都有。

Chinese food has all kinds of flavors: sour, sweet, bitter, and spicy.

红黄蓝绿, 各种颜色的衣服她都有。

She has clothes in all kinds of colors such as red, yellow, blue, and green.

Note: The example from the text, 酸甜苦辣, has become a fixed expression to indicate all kinds of flavors.

6. V得惯 able to get used to something

Negative form: V不惯   unable to get used to something

Question form: Object, V得惯V不惯

This is the potential complement form, emphasizing one's potential or ability to get used to something/doing something. The resultative complement forms are:

V惯了   have gotten used to something

没V惯   haven't gotten used to something

Question form: V惯了没有

▶ 中国菜你吃得惯吃不惯？

Are you able to get used to eating Chinese food?

美国人喝不惯热水。

Americans are not able to get used to drinking hot water.

The topic of this structure, that is, 中国菜 and 热水 in the two above examples, can be put at the beginning of the sentence or after the verb in the regular object position.

7. 习惯 + V.P. (used to doing something)

In Lesson 9 "喝茶还是喝咖啡" we learned 习惯 used as a noun, that is, habit. In this lesson, it is used as a verb. It emphasizes the state of being used to something. 习惯 and V得惯 have similar meanings, but structurally they are different. V得惯 is the potential complement form, so it emphasizes the potential for someone to get used to something. Furthermore, when there is a modifier, such as "比较" in the following example, it is better to use 习惯.

▶ 我还是比较习惯用刀叉。

I am still more used to using knife and fork.

中国人习惯喝热水。

Chinese are used to drinking hot water.

Cultural Notes

Chinatown in the United States
美国的中国城

With the first wave of Chinese immigrants coming to the United States in the late nineteenth century to work as laborers in the mining industry and on the transcontinental railroad, Chinatown, as an ethnic enclave of Chinese people in America, gradually came into being. The ebb and flow of Chinatowns in the United States over the past century reflects the changes in policy and attitude of the American government and society toward Chinese immigration.

There are many Chinatowns scattered throughout the United States. Some of the most famous and prosperous ones include those in San Francisco, New York City, and Chicago, where you can see ancient-style red arch entrances, bilingual signs, numerous Chinese restaurants, and small shops selling interesting Chinese products, such as traditional Chinese medicines.

Most of the early residents of Chinatowns in the United States were people from Guangdong and Fujian provinces in China; therefore Guangdong hua 广东话 (Cantonese) has been the dominant language for decades. In recent years, with more and more young immigrants coming from other parts of China, Cantonese is being rapidly replaced by Putonghua 普通话 (Mandarin Chinese).

Besides being a tourist attraction and a center for overseas Chinese, Chinatown is also a place where people live and work. It is typically considered a shelter for "recent immigrants and unskilled laborers who do not have good English proficiency" (see the entry on "Chinatown" in Wikipedia, http://en.wikipedia.org/wiki/Chinatown). Such a role has made Chinatowns quite vulnerable and has limited their development over time.

Traditional Character Text

中國城

（A——張三，B——小丁）

A：小丁，上個週末你到哪兒去了？

B：我和同屋去了一次紐約的中國城。

A：你們是怎麼去的？是坐汽車去的，還是坐火車去的？

B：我們是坐火車去的。

A：爲什麼不坐公共汽車呢？

B：因爲路上常常堵車，可是火車沒有這個問題，而且火車比汽車快。

A：可是火車並不到中國城啊。

B：到了紐約的火車站，轉一次地鐵就到中國城了，挺方便的。

A：你在中國城說中國話了嗎？

B：我們去了一家中國飯館兒，我跟服務員說普通話，但是服務員跟我說英文。開始我以爲他聽不懂我的中文，讓我挺失望的；後來我才知道，很多飯館兒的服務員只會說廣東話，不會說普通話。到了紐約的中國城，我才知道，"普通話"並不"普通"。

A：你喜歡那家飯館兒的菜嗎？

B：我點了一個雞肉，有點兒辣。我的同屋點了一條魚，是帶頭的，看起來有點兒奇怪，可是吃起來好吃極了。

A：中國菜都是辣的嗎？

B：不是，有的辣，有的不辣。中國菜，酸甜苦辣，各種味道都有。上海菜沒有北京菜那麼咸。上海人做菜的時候，鹽放得不多，喜歡放醋和糖，所以上海菜又酸又甜。

A：中國菜你吃得慣吃不慣？

B：中國菜吃得慣，可是筷子用不慣。我還是比較習慣用刀叉。

A：下次你去中國城的時候，給我打個電話，我也去。

B：沒問題。

CHAPTER 20

Dōngyà Túshū Guǎn
(East Asian Library)

Pinyin Text

Xuéxiào lǐ yǒu ge Dōngyà túshū guǎn, jiù zài Dōngyà xì de lóushàng. Wǒ zuì xǐhuān zài nàr kànshū xuéxí. Zhèige túshūguǎn bìng búdà, zàinàr kànshū de rén hěnshǎo, jiè shū huán shū de rén yě bù duō, suǒyǐ hěn ānjìng.

Túshūguǎn de qiángshang guàzhe jǐfú Zhōngguó de zìhuà, wǒ suīrán kànbudǒng xiě de shì shénme, dànshì wǒ hěn xǐhuān nèifú shānshuǐ huà. Shūjià shang bǎizhe chéngqiānshàngwàn de Zhōngwén shū, kěxī wǒ lián yìběn dōu kànbudǒng. Yàoshì yǒuyìtiān wǒ kàndedǒng Zhōngwén shū le, nà gāi duōhǎo a !

English Translation

There is an East Asian Library on the floor above the Department of East Asian Studies. I like reading and studying there the most. This library is actually not that big. There are few people reading. There are not many people borrowing or returning books either, so it is quiet there.

There are a few Chinese calligraphy and paintings hanging on the wall of the library. Although I cannot understand what is written on them, I like that landscape painting very much. There are tens of thousands of books displayed on the bookshelves, but it's a shame I cannot understand even one. If one day I were able to read books in Chinese, how great that would be!

东亚	東亞	Dōngyà	n.	East Asia
图书馆	圖書館	túshūguǎn	n.	library
系		xì	n.	department
楼上		lóushàng	adv.	upstairs
学习	學習	xuéxí	v.	to learn, to study
借		jiè	v.	to borrow
还	還	huán	v.	to return (an object), to give back
安静	安靜	ānjìng	adj.	quiet

第二十课 东亚图书馆

　　学校里有个东亚图书馆，就在东亚系的楼上，我最喜欢在那儿看书学习。这个图书馆并不大，在那儿看书的人很少，借书还书的人也不多，所以很安静。

　　图书馆的墙上挂着几幅中国的字画儿，我虽然看不懂写的是什么，但是我很喜欢那幅山水画儿。书架上摆着成千上万的中文书，可惜我连一本都看不懂。要是有一天我看得懂中文书了，那该多好啊！

挂	掛	guà	v.	to hang, to put up
幅		fú	m.w.	measure word for paintings
字画(儿)	字畫(兒)	zìhuà(r)	n.	calligraphy and painting
山水画(儿)	山水畫(兒)	shānshuǐhuà(r)	n.	landscape painting
书架	書架	shūjià	n.	bookcase, bookshelf
摆	擺	bǎi	v.	to put, to place, to arrange
成千上万	成千上萬	chéngqiānshàngwàn	phrase	tens of thousands
可惜		kěxī	adj.	It's a pity that …

Zài yuèlǎnshì lǐ, kànbào de rén bǐ kànshū de rén duō. Yǒude zuòzhe kàn, yǒude zhànzhe kàn. Suīrán xuéxiào guīdìng bù kěyǐ zài túshūguǎn lǐ dǎ diànhuà, kěshì hái yǒu rén yìbiān kàn shū, yìbiān dǎ diànhuà hé péngyou liáotiānr. Zhè ràng wǒ fēicháng shēngqì.

Wǒmen xuéxiào de Dōngyà túshūguǎn hěn yǒumíng, yǒu hěnduō Zhōngguó gǔdài de shū. Zhèixiē shū zài qítā dìfang dōu yǐjīng zhǎobúdào le. Xuéxiào lǐ yǒu zhèyàng yíge túshūguǎn, lǎoshī hé xuéshēng dōu juéde hěn fāngbiàn.

In the reading room, there are more people reading newspapers than reading books. Some sit there reading, and some stand there reading. Although the school has a rule that no phone calls should be made in the library, there are still some people who chat with friends on the phone while reading. This makes me very angry.

The East Asian Library of our university is well-known. There are plenty of ancient Chinese books. These books cannot be found anywhere else. Both teachers and students think that it is very convenient to have such a library on campus.

阅览室	閱覽室	yuèlǎnshì	n.	reading room
看报	看報	kànbào	v.o.	to read newspaper
规定	規定	guīdìng	n./v.	regulations; to make regulations
一边儿(邊兒)……一边儿		yìbiān(r)	conj.	doing one thing while doing another
聊天(儿)		liáotiān(r)	v.o.	to chat

在阅览室里，看报的人比看书的人多。有的坐着看，有的站着看。虽然学校规定不可以在图书馆里打电话，可是还有人一边看书，一边打电话和朋友聊天儿。这让我非常生气。

我们学校的东亚图书馆很有名，有很多中国古代的书。这些书在其他地方都已经找不到了。学校里有这样一个图书馆，老师和学生都觉得很方便。

生气	生氣	shēngqì	v.	to take offense, to get angry
有名		yǒumíng	adj.	famous
古代		gǔdài	n.	ancient times
其他		qítā	adj.	the rest, other, else
地方		dìfāng	n.	place, space

语法 Grammar Notes

1. 就 (adv.) (just)

Here 就 is used as an emphatic marker. When it is followed by "在 + place word" it indicates that the location isn't far away.

▶ 学校里有个东亚图书馆，就在东亚系的楼上。

There is an East Asian Library right on the floor above the Department of East Asian Studies.

我不知道你就在我后边。

I didn't know you were just behind me.

2. 着 (verb suffix)

(1) Location + verb + 着 + noun

This pattern indicates a static state of existence. Verbs often used in this pattern include 挂 guà (to hang), 摆 bǎi (to display), 放 fàng (to put), 坐 zuò (to sit), 站 zhàn (to stand), 躺 tǎng (to lie on one's back), 趴 pā (to lie on one's stomach).

▶ 图书馆的墙上挂着几幅中国的字画儿。

There are a few Chinese calligraphy and paintings hanging on the wall of the library.

▶ 书架上摆着成千上万的中文书。

There are tens of thousands of Chinese books displayed on the bookshelves.

(2) Subject + verb + 着 (+ object)

We use this pattern to describe the state a person or an object is in. For example:

门开着。　　　　The door is open.
他穿着红衣服。　He's wearing red clothes.

(3) Subject + verb 1 着 (+ object 1) + verb 2 (+ object 2)

We use this pattern to describe the state or manner in which an action is carried out. More specifically, the first verbal pattern with 着 modifies the second.

▶ 有的坐着看，有的站着看。

Some people sit there reading, and some stand there reading.

老师站着跟我们说话。
The teacher stood there talking to us.

3. 可惜 + sentence (it is a shame that … ; it's a pity that …)

▶ 书架上摆着成千上万的中文书，可惜我连一本都看不懂。
There are tens of thousands of Chinese books displayed on the bookshelves; it's a shame that I cannot understand even one.

今天天气很好，可惜我们的作业太多不能出去。
The weather is good today. It's a shame that we have too much homework and cannot go out.

4. 该 (should)

(1) 该 can be used as an auxiliary verb, a shortened form of "应该."

该起床了。
(You) should get up.

昨天我不该去纽约。
I should not have gone to New York yesterday.

(2) When used in the structure "要是……, (那) 该多好啊," it suggests a strong wish: How nice it would/should be if. …

▶ 要是有一天我看得懂中文书了，那该多好啊！
How great it would be if I were able to read Chinese books someday!

要是我夏天能去北京，那该多好啊！
It would be great if I could go to Beijing in the summer!

5. 其他(的) + noun (other, else)

When modifying a monosyllabic noun, it is usually followed by 的. Otherwise, 的 is often optional.

▶ 这些书在其他地方已经找不到了。
These books already cannot be found elsewhere.

除了我以外，其他的人都知道东亚图书馆在哪儿。
Except for me, the others all know where the East Asian library is.

6. Subject 一边V.P.1, 一边V.P.2 (doing one thing while doing another)

▶有人一边看书，一边打电话和朋友聊天儿。
Some chat with their friends on the phone while reading.

他一边吃饭，一边做作业。
He is doing his homework while eating.

Traditional Character Text

東亞圖書館

　　學校裏有個東亞圖書館，就在東亞系的樓上，我最喜歡在那兒看書學習。這個圖書館並不大，在那兒看書的人很少，借書還書的人也不多，所以很安靜。

　　圖書館的牆上掛著幾幅中國的字畫兒，我雖然看不懂寫的是什麼，但是我很喜歡那幅山水畫兒。書架上擺著成千上萬的中文書，可惜我連一本都看不懂。要是有一天我看得懂中文書了，那該多好啊！

　　在閱覽室裏，看報的人比看書的人多。有的坐著看，有的站著看。雖然學校規定不可以在圖書館裏打電話，可是還有人一邊看書，一邊打電話和朋友聊天兒。這讓我非常生氣。

　　我們學校的東亞圖書館很有名，有很多中國古代的書。這些書在其他地方都已經找不到了。學校裏有這樣一個圖書館，老師和學生都覺得很方便。

21 Zhōngwén Zhuōzi (Chinese Table)

Pinyin Text

Měige xīngqīsì wǎnshàng liùdiǎn, wǒmen sùshè de cāntīng dōu yǒu yícì Zhōngwén zhuōzi de huódòng. Lǎoshī hé tóngxuémen zuò zài yìqǐ chī wǎnfàn. Dàjiā yìbiān chīfàn, yìbiān shuō Zhōngwén, yǒu yìsi jíle. Wǒ zài Zhōngwén zhuōzi xuédào le hěnduō zài jiàoshì lǐ xuébúdào de dōngxi, xiàng cài, yǐnliào hé tiándiǎn de míngzi, dōushì cóng Zhōngwén zhuōzi xuélái de. Shàngkè de shíhòu, suīrán yě gēn lǎoshī tánhuà, dànshì hěnshǎo yǒu jīhuì tándào gèrén de shì. Chīfàn de shíhòu, wǒmen chángcháng tándào zìjǐ de jiārén hé xiǎoshíhou de shìqing. Lǎoshī men yǒude shì cóng Zhōngguó dàlù lái de, yǒude shì cóng Táiwān láide. Tāmen búdàn kǒuyīn yǒuxiē bùtóng, duì hěnduō wèntí de kànfǎ yě bùtóng.

English Translation

Every Thursday night at six o'clock there is a Chinese Table event in the cafeteria in our dorm. Teachers and students sit together to have dinner. Everyone speaks Chinese while they are eating. It is extremely interesting. At the Chinese Table, I have learned a lot of things that cannot be learned in the classroom: the names of the dishes, drinks, and desserts were all learned at Chinese Table. When we have class, although we also talk with our teachers, we seldom have the chance to talk about personal affairs. When we eat, we often talk about our own families and things that happened during our childhoods. Among the teachers, some are from Mainland China, and some are from Taiwan. Not only are their accents somewhat different, but their opinions on many topics are also different.

餐厅	餐廳	cāntīng	n.	cafeteria, restaurant
活动	活動	huódòng	n.	activity, event
一起		yìqǐ	adv.	together
大家		dàjiā	pron.	everybody

第二十一课 中文桌子

每个星期四晚上6点，我们宿舍的餐厅都有一次中文桌子的活动。老师和同学们坐在一起吃晚饭。大家一边吃饭，一边说中文，有意思极了。我在中文桌子学到了很多在教室里学不到的东西，像菜、饮料和甜点的名字，都是从中文桌子学来的。上课的时候，虽然也跟老师谈话，但是很少有机会谈到个人的事。吃饭的时候，我们常常谈到自己的家人和小时候的事情。老师们有的是从中国大陆来的，有的是从台湾来的。他们不但口音有些不同，对很多问题的看法也不同。

学到	學到	xuédào	v.c.	to learn
饮料	飲料	yǐnliào	n.	soft drinks
谈话	談話	tánhuà	v./n.	to talk; talk
机会	機會	jīhuì	n.	chance, opportunity
个人	個人	gèrén	n./adj.	individual; personal
小时候	小時候	xiǎoshíhòu	n.	childhood
事情		shìqíng	n.	events, matters
大陆	大陸	dàlù	n.	mainland
台湾	臺灣	Táiwān	n.	Taiwan
口音		kǒuyīn	n.	accent
看法		kànfǎ	n.	opinion

Wǒ zuìpà hé gāo niánjí de xuéshēng zuòzài yìqǐ chī Zhōngwén zhuōzi. Tāmen shuōhuà shuō de hěnkuài, wǒ chángcháng tīngbudǒng; dànshì Lǎoshī zhīdào wǒmen de shuǐpíng, tāmen shuō de hěnmàn, yě shuōde hěn qīngchǔ.

Suīrán wǒmen bǎ zhèige huódòng jiàozuò Zhōngwén zhuōzi, dànshì wǒmen chīde háishì Měiguó cài, bìng búshì Zhōngguó cài, zhè ràng wǒ yǒuxiē shīwàng.

I am most afraid of sitting together with students from higher levels when I eat at Chinese Table. They speak very fast, and I often do not understand them; however, the teachers know our level. They speak slowly and very clearly.

Although we call this activity "Chinese Table," we still eat American dishes, not actual Chinese dishes. This makes me somewhat disappointed.

年级	年級	niánjí	n.	grade, level
水平		shuǐpíng	n.	level

我最怕和高年级的学生坐在一起吃中文桌子。他们说话说得很快，我常常听不懂；但是老师知道我们的水平，他们说得很慢，也说得很清楚。

虽然我们把这个活动叫做中文桌子，但是我们吃的还是美国菜，并不是中国菜，这让我有些失望。

语法 Grammar Notes

1. 学到 (to learn, to have learned)

Positive potential form: 学得到 can learn
Negative potential form: 学不到 cannot learn

到 as a verb complement emphasizes the result of the action. For example,

学 to study   学到 to learn
看 to look   看到 to see
听 to listen   听到 to hear
找 to look for   找到 to find
谈 to talk about, to chat 谈到 to touch on the topic of

▶ 我在中文桌子学到了很多在教室里学不到的东西。
At Chinese Table, I have learned many things that I cannot learn in the classroom.

▶ 上课的时候，我们很少有机会谈到个人的事。
When we have class, we seldom have the chance to talk about personal affairs.

在中国的时候，我看到了很多在美国没看到过的事.
When I was in China, I saw many things that I have not seen in the United States.

2. 有机会 (to have an opportunity)

Subject 有机会 V.   to have the opportunity to do something

有机会 Subject (会/要) V.   If there is an opportunity, … ("if" is deleted in the Chinese version of this sentence.)

In the second sentence pattern, the position of the subject is movable. It can also be placed at the beginning of the sentence. You may sometimes find 会/要 before the main verbs to indicate future actions.

中国大陆的人很少有机会去台湾。
People from Mainland China seldom have the chance to go to Taiwan.

有机会我想去北京学中文。
[If] there is an opportunity, I want to go to Beijing to study Chinese.

3. Review 有的

有的 (noun). + V.1/adj.1, 有的 (noun) + V.2/adj.2   some … some …
or
Pronoun/Noun 有的 V.1/adj.1, 有的 V.2/adj.2

This structure describes different parts of an entire body of things or people. One may put the noun after 有的 (the noun is optional when it is understood in context), or put the pronoun or noun before 有的 to indicate the scope.

▶ 老师们有的是从大陆来的，有的是从台湾来的。
Some of the teachers are from Mainland China, and some are from Taiwan.

有的人喜欢看书，有的人喜欢运动。
Some people like to read, and some like to exercise.

4. 对…… 的看法   opinion of something/somebody

▶ 他们不但口音有些不同，对很多问题的看法也不同。
Not only are their accents somewhat different, but their opinions on many topics are also different.

你对这个问题有什么看法？
What is your opinion on this topic?

5. 把 A 叫做 B (to call A as B)

A and B are noun phrases. They can refer to people or things.

▶ 我们把这个活动叫做中文桌子。
We call this activity Chinese Table.

中国人常常把美国人叫做"老美"。
Chinese people often call Americans "old American."

Traditional Character Text

中文桌子

　　每個星期四晚上6點，我們宿舍的餐廳都有一次中文桌子的活動。老師和同學們坐在一起吃晚飯。大家一邊吃飯，一邊說中文，有意思極了。我在中文桌子學到了很多在教室裏學不到的東西，像菜、飲料和甜點的名字，都是從中文桌子學來的。上課的時候，雖然也跟老師談話，但是很少有機會談到個人的事。吃飯的時候，我們常常談到自己的家人和小時候的事情。老師們有的是從中國大陸來的，有的是從臺灣來的。他們不但口音有些不同，對很多問題的看法也不同。

　　我最怕和高年級的學生坐在一起吃中文桌子。他們說話說得很快，我常常聽不懂；但是老師知道我們的水平，他們說得很慢，也說得很清楚。

　　雖然我們把這個活動叫做中文桌子，但是我們吃的還是美國菜，並不是中國菜，這讓我有些失望。

Wǒmen de Zhōngwén Lǎoshī
(Our Chinese Teachers)

Pinyin Text

Zhèixuéqī wǒmen yǒu qīwèi Zhōngwén lǎoshī. Dàduō shì nǚ lǎoshī, zhǐyǒu liǎngwèi nán lǎoshī. Tāmen yǒude shì cóng Běijīng lái de, yǒude shì cóng Shànghǎi láide, yě yǒu yíwèi shì cóng Táiwān lái de. Jùshuō Běijīng lǎoshī shuō de Zhōngwén gēn Shànghǎi lǎoshī shuō de yǒudiǎnr bùtóng, kěshì wǒ wánquán tīng bu chūlái shéi shì cóng Běijīng láide, shéi shì cóng Shànghǎi lái de. Wǒ juéde tāmen shuō de Zhōngwén dōu chàbuduō, wǒ dōu tīng bútài dǒng.

Liǎngwèi nán lǎoshī kànqǐlái niánjì bǐjiào dà. Yíwèi dàgài sìshí suì, yíwèi dàgài wǔshí jǐ suì. Niánjì zuìdà de nèiwèi lǎoshī, lián tóufa dōu báile, kěshì hái tǐngyǒu jīngshén de. Nǚ lǎoshī dōu hěn niánqīng, tāmen dōu hái búdào sānshí suì. Yǒude gèzi gāo, yǒude gèzi ǎi.

English Translation

We have seven Chinese teachers this semester. Most of them are female teachers; only two are male. Some of them come from Beijing, some from Shanghai, and there is another one from Taiwan. It is said that teachers from Beijing speak Chinese a little differently from Shanghai teachers; however, I can't tell at all who comes from Beijing and who comes from Shanghai by listening to them speak. I think the way Chinese people speak is pretty much the same; and I can't really understand them.

The two male teachers look older. One is about forty years old, and one is a little over fifty. As for the most senior teacher, even his hair is white; but he is still very energetic. The female teachers are all very young. They are all less than thirty years old. Some of them are tall and some are short.

第二十二课 我们的中文老师

　　这学期我们有七位中文老师。大多是女老师，只有两位男老师。他们有的是从北京来的，有的是从上海来的，也有一位是从台湾来的。据说北京老师说的中文跟上海老师说的有点儿不同，可是我完全听不出来谁是从北京来的，谁是从上海来的。我觉得他们说的中文都差不多，我都听不太懂。

　　两位男老师看起来年纪比较大。一位大概40岁，一位大概50几岁。年纪最大的那位老师，连头发都白了，可是还挺有精神的。女老师都很年轻，她们都还不到30岁。有的个子高，有的个子矮。

据说		jùshuō	phrase	It's said that …
年纪	年紀	niánjì	n.	age (can be modified by 大/小, e.g., 年纪大, 年纪小, 多大年纪?)
大概		dàgài	adv.	approximately; probably
有精神		yǒujīngshén	phrase	having spirit, energetic
年轻	年輕	niánqīng	adj.	young
个子	個子	gèzi	n.	height (of a person)

Tāmen dōuhěn piàoliang, yě hěn héqì. Wǒ zuì xǐhuān hé tāmen tánhuà. Tánhuà de shíhou, tāmen búdàn shì wǒde lǎoshī, yěshì wǒde péngyou.

Wǒ zuì xǐhuān de nèiwèi lǎoshī, tóufa chángcháng de, yǎnjing dàdà de, bízi gāogāo de, zuǐba xiǎoxiǎo de. Tā bùgāo bùǎi, búpàng búshòu, jiù xiàng wǒ jiějie. Wǒ xīwàng měitiān dōu néng gēn tā shàngkè, gēn tā tánhuà.

Zhǐyǒu yíwèi lǎoshī wǒ bútài xǐhuān. Tā cónglái búxiào, kànqǐlái hěn bù gāoxìng. Tā shuōhuà de shēngyīn hěnxiǎo. Wǒ búshì tīng bu qīngchǔ jiùshì tīngbudǒng tā shuō de huà. Wǒ zuì pà shàng tāde kè.

They are all very pretty and also very polite. I like to talk with them the most. When we talk, they are not only my teachers, but also my friends.

My favorite teacher is the one with long hair, big eyes, a tall nose, and a small mouth. She is neither tall nor short, neither fat nor skinny, just like my older sister. I wish I could have class and talk with her every day.

There is only one teacher whom I don't really like. She never smiles and looks very unhappy. Her voice is very soft. I either can't hear her clearly or can't understand what she says. I am most afraid of attending her class.

和气	和氣	héqì	adj.	polite, friendly, nice
头发	頭髮	tóufa	n.	hair
鼻子		bízi	n.	nose

她们都很漂亮，也很和气。我最喜欢和她们谈话。谈话的时候，她们不但是我的老师，也是我的朋友。

我最喜欢的那位老師，头发长长的，眼睛大大的，鼻子高高的，嘴巴小小的。她不高不矮，不胖不瘦，就像我姐姐。我希望每天都能跟她上课，跟她谈话。

只有一位老师我不太喜欢。她从来不笑，看起来很不高兴。她说话的声音很小，我不是听不清楚就是听不懂她说的话。我最怕上她的课。

嘴巴		zuǐbā	n.	mouth
希望		xīwàng	v.	to hope
从来(不/没有)	從來	cónglái	adv.	never
笑		xiào	v.	to laugh
声音	聲音	shēngyīn	n.	voice

语法 Grammar Notes

1. 只有 (only have; there is only ...)

Because 有 has meanings of both ownership and existence in Chinese, accordingly 只有 also has these two indications.

▶ 大多是女老师，只有两位男老师。

Most of them are female teachers. There are only two male teachers.

他只有一个中国朋友。

He has only one Chinese friend.

教室里只有一把椅子。

There is only one chair in the classroom.

只有 can also be used as a conjunction "only," and in this case it is always put at the beginning of a sentence. What is followed immediately by 只有 is the topic that the speaker wants to emphasize.

只有 **somebody/something + (subject) + V.**

▶ 只有一位老师我不太喜欢。

There is only one teacher whom I don't like very much.

只有那位男老师头发白了。

Only that male teacher's hair has turned white.

2. 据说 (It is said ...)

▶ 据说北京老师说的中文跟上海老师说的有点儿不同。

It is said that teachers from Beijing speak Chinese a little differently from Shanghai teachers.

To identify the source of information, you can use 据 somebody/something 说: according to somebody or some source.

据报纸说，越来越多的美国人学中文。

According to the newspaper, more and more Americans study Chinese.

Note: you CANNOT say "我据说......"

3. 出来 (used as a verb complement)

V + 出来 indicates perception or recognition of something by seeing, hearing, or some other method. The potential complement forms are:

听得出来 be able to recognize by listening (negative form: 听不出来)
看得出来 be able to recognize by looking (negative form: 看不出来)

Their resultative complement forms are:

听出来了 recognized by listening (negative form: 没听出来)
看出来了 recognized by looking (negative form: 没看出来)

我听不出来这位老师是台湾人。
I cannot recognize that this teacher is Taiwanese by listening to her speaking.

我看不出来这是什么字。
I cannot recognize this character by looking at it.

The complement structure can also be "split," which means to insert the object between 出 and 来. So the previous two examples can also be:

我听不出这位老师是台湾人(来)。
我看不出这是什么字(来)。

The split complement has exactly the same meaning as the unsplit form. All forms of the complement 出来 (potential and resultative) have equivalent unsplit and split versions. 来 is optional and can be dropped, especially when the insertion is long in the split form.

4. 大概 vs. 可能

Both 大概 and 可能 can be used before a sentence or in between a subject and a predicate, meaning "perhaps, maybe." In this case, they are interchangeable.

▶ 可能是住在附近的孩子偷的。
It probably was some kid from the neighborhood who stole the bike.

(可能 in this sentence can be replaced with 大概. The meaning of the sentence does not change at all.)

However, 大概 can be used before numbers, meaning "approximately," while 也许 cannot.

这双球鞋大概50元。 This pair of sneakers is about fifty dollars.
那位老师大概40岁。 The teacher is about forty years old.

5. Review: 连······ 都······ (even)

For a detailed explanation, refer to grammar note 11 of Lesson 11. There are two basic patterns:

连 **subject** 都 **verb**

Subject 连 **object** 都 **verb**

The following are examples of each pattern, respectively:

▶ 那位老师年纪很大，连头发都白了。

That teacher is quite old; his hair has even turned white.

他连"大"字都不会写。

He can't even write the character "dà."

6. Reduplication of Monosyllabic Adjectives (i.e., A A 的)

This structure is used to make the description more lively and vivid. The adjective has to be in its original form and may NOT be used with 很, 非常, or other adverbial modifiers.

▶ 她的头发长长的，眼睛大大的，鼻子高高的，嘴巴小小的。

Her hair is long, her eyes are big, her nose is high, and her mouth is small.

7. Subject 希望 + Clause (to wish that/to hope that ...)

希望 can be used as a verb and as a noun to mean "to hope" and "hope," respectively. When it is used as a verb it can be followed by a clause or a verb phrase.

Subject 希望 + **clause** **Subject** 希望 + **V.P.**

▶ 我希望每天都能跟她上课。

I wish that I could have class with her every day.

As an emotion verb, 希望 can be modified by 很, 非常, 真, and so on.

他真希望能去中国学中文。

He really hopes that he can go to China to study Chinese.

8. **Review: 就 adv. (just; exactly (emphatic))**

▶ 那位老师就像我姐姐。

That teacher is just like my older sister.

那个带着眼镜的老师就是周老师。

The teacher who wears glasses is none other than Teacher Zhou.

9. 从来 (都) 不 V.　　　　never do something (habitual action)
　从来 (都) 没 (有) V. 过　have never done something (past experience)

从来 "have (never)" typically is followed by a negative. Using 不 with 从来 indicates habitual action, suggesting that the speaker has a kind of policy or habit that has prevented action in the past and probably will continue to do so in the future. You can also emphasize past experience by using 没有V.过 with 从来. This indicates that the action has not happened in the past, although it might happen in the future.

▶ 她从来不笑。　　　　　　She never smiles.
　他从来都没去过台湾。　　He has never been to Taiwan.

Traditional Character Text

我們的中文老師

這學期我們有七位中文老師。大多是女老師，只有兩位男老師。他們有的是從北京來的，有的是從上海來的，也有一位是從臺灣來的。據說北京老師說的中文跟上海老師說的有點兒不同，可是我完全聽不出來誰是從北京來的，誰是從上海來的。我覺得他們說的中文都差不多，我都聽不太懂。

兩位男老師看起來年紀比較大。一位大概40歲，一位大概50幾歲。年紀最大的那位老師，連頭髮都白了，可是還挺有精神的。女老師都很年輕，她們都還不到30歲。有的個子高，有的個子矮。

她們都很漂亮，也很和氣。我最喜歡和她們談話。談話的時候，她們不但是我的老師，也是我的朋友。

我最喜歡的那位老師，頭髮長長的，眼睛大大的，鼻子高高的，嘴巴小小的。她不高不矮，不胖不瘦，就像我姐姐。我希望每天都能跟她上課，跟她談話。

只有一位老師我不太喜歡。她從來不笑，看起來很不高興。她說話的聲音很小，我不是聽不清楚就是聽不懂她說的話。我最怕上她的課。

Pinyin Text

Lǎoshī men wèile ràng dàjiā yǒu liànxí shuō Zhōngwén de jīhuì, ānpái měige tóngxué měi liǎngge xīngqī hé lǎoshī jiàn yícì miàn. Jiànmiàn de shíhou, kěyǐ tántan shàngkè de shíhou bùnéng tán de huàtí. Wǒmen bǎ zhèige huódòng jiào zuò "gèbié tánhuà." Wǒ zuì xǐhuān gèbié tánhuà, yīnwèi gèbié tánhuà hěn qīngsōng, xuédào de dōngxi yě hěnduō.

Wǒ hé Wáng lǎoshī zuì tándelái. Shàngkè de shíhou, wǒmen shì lǎoshī hé xuéshēng, gèbié tánhuà de shíhou, wǒmen shì hǎo péngyou. Wǒmen cóng jiālǐ de shìqing tán dào xuéxí de shìqing, cóng xué Zhōngwén tán dào xué Yīngwén. Yǐqián wǒ juéde Yīngwén hěn róngyì, hé Wáng lǎoshī tánhuà yǐhòu cái fāxiàn xué Yīngwén duì Zhōngguórén lái shuō hěnnán.

English Translation

Teachers arrange to have each student meet with them once every two weeks so that we can have an opportunity to practice speaking Chinese. When we meet, we can talk about topics that we cannot talk about in class. We call this activity "individual sessions." I like individual sessions the best because they are very relaxing, and I also learn a lot.

I get along best with Teacher Wang. In class, we are teacher and student, but in individual sessions we are good friends. We talk about topics ranging from family to study, from learning Chinese to learning English. I used to think that English was easy, but after talking to Teacher Wang, I realized that learning English is very hard for Chinese people.

| 个别 | 個別 | gèbié | adj./adv. | individual; individually |
| 个别谈话 | 個別談話 | gèbié tánhuà | phrase | individual sessions; to have individual sessions |

第二十三课 个别谈话

老师们为了让大家有练习说中文的机会，安排每个同学每两个星期和老师见一次面。见面的时候，可以谈谈上课的时候不能谈的话题。我们把这个活动叫做"个别谈话"。我最喜欢个别谈话，因为个别谈话很轻松，学到的东西也很多。

我和王老师最谈得来。上课的时候，我们是老师和学生，个别谈话的时候，我们是好朋友。我们从家里的事情谈到学习的事情，从学中文谈到学英文。以前我觉得英文很容易，和王老师谈话以后才发现，学英文对中国人来说很难。

为了	為了	wèile	prep.	for, in order to, for the sake of
练习	練習	liànxí	v.	to practice
安排		ānpái	v.	to arrange
见面	見面	jiànmiàn	v.o.	to meet
话题	話題	huàtí	n.	topic
谈得来	談得來	tándelái	v.c.	to be able to get along well (negative form: 谈不来)
发现	發現	fāxiàn	v.	to discover, to realize
对……来说	對……來說	duì … láishuō	phrase	to somebody, as for somebody

Lǎoshī men dōu hěn zhùyì wǒmen de fāyīn. Zhōngwén de fāyīn hěn nán, dànshì yě hěn zhòngyào. Yàoshì fāyīn búduì, jiù huì nào hěn dà de xiàohua. Zài fànguǎnr lǐ, qiānwàn bùnéng bǎ "shuǐjiǎo" shuōchéng "shuìjiào." Yàoshì yíge nán xuéshēng wèn yíge nǚ fúwùyuán de shíhou, bǎ "Shuǐjiǎo yìwǎn duōshǎoqián? " shuōchéng "Shuìjiào yìwǎn duōshǎoqián?" tā kěnéng huì yǒu hěndà de máfan.

Měicì gèbié tánhuà zhǐyǒu shíwǔ fēnzhōng, wǒ juéde tài duǎn le. Dànshì duì lǎoshī lái shuō, shíwǔ fēnzhōng bìng bùduǎn, yīnwèi tāmen měige xīngqī dōu děi gēn hěnduō xuéshēng tánhuà.

The teachers all pay close attention to our pronunciation. Chinese pronunciation is very difficult but also very important. If your pronunciation is incorrect, you will make a big fool of yourself. When you are in a restaurant, be sure not to pronounce "shuǐjiǎo" as "shuìjiào." If, when speaking to a waitress, a male student tries to say, "How much is a bowl of dumplings?" and it comes out as "How much does it cost to sleep with you for a night?" he will probably be in big trouble.

Each individual session is only 15 minutes long. I feel that that's too short. But it's not short for the teachers, because they have individual sessions with many students every week.

注意		zhùyì	v.	to pay attention to
发音	發音	fāyīn	n./v.o.	pronunciation; to pronounce
笑话	笑話	xiàohuà	n.	joke
闹笑话	鬧笑話	nàoxiàohuà	v.o.	to make a fool of oneself
千万	千萬	qiānwàn	adv.	(of an admonition) be sure (not) to
水饺	水餃	shuǐjiǎo	n.	dumplings with soup
说成	説成	shuōchéng	v.	to (mistakenly) say something as

老师们都很注意我们的发音。中文的发音很难，但是也很重要。要是发音不对，就会闹很大的笑话。在饭馆儿里，千万不能把"水饺"说成"睡觉"。要是一个男学生问一个女服务员的时候，把"水饺一碗多少钱？"说成"睡觉一晚多少钱？"他可能会有很大的麻烦。

每次个别谈话只有15分钟，我觉得太短了。但是，对老师来说，15分钟并不短，因为他们每个星期都得跟很多学生谈话。

碗		wǎn	n./m.w.	bowl; a bowl of
晚		wǎn	n.	night
麻烦	麻烦	máfán	n.	trouble

语法 Grammar Notes

1. 为了 (for the purpose of, for the sake of)

为了 can be followed by a noun or by a verb phrase. It is often placed at the beginning of a sentence.

▶ 老师们为了让大家有练习说中文的机会，安排每个同学每两个星期和老师见一次面。

Teachers arrange to have each student meet with them once every two weeks so that we can have an opportunity to practice speaking Chinese.

为了准备考试，我天天去图书馆学习。

In order to prepare for the exam, I go to study in the library every day.

2. Review 每 (every, each)

每 is often followed by measure word + noun, such as 每个学生 (every student) and 每个人 (everybody). However, if the noun also behaves like a measure word, it does not require another measure word in the pattern. 每天 (every day) and 每年 (měinián, every year) are such examples. 每 can also be used to express frequency:

每 + time duration + verb + num. + 次 + object

▶ 学生每两个星期和中文老师见一次面。

The students meet with the Chinese teachers once every two weeks.

3. 安排 (to arrange)

安排 can take nouns as its direct objects. Some possible combinations with words that we have learned include:

安排时间	to manage time, to arrange time
(给学生)安排宿舍	to arrange dorms (for the students)
(给学生) 安排教室	to arrange classrooms (for the students)

A common pattern of 安排:

安排 + somebody + V.P.
to arrange someone to do …

老师安排我们下个星期考试。
The teacher arranged for us to take the examination next week.

4. (Subject) V.P. 的时候 (when/while)

▶ 见面的时候，可以谈谈上课的时候不能谈的话题。
When we meet, we can talk about topics that we cannot talk about in class.

上课的时候，我们是老师和学生，个别谈话的时候，我们是朋友。
While having class, we are teacher and student; but while having individual sessions, we are friends.

5. Reduplication of Monosyllabic Verbs (AA)

Reduplication makes the action seem more relaxing and enjoyable, and also softens the tone of the speaker. For example,

试试	to have a try
谈谈	to chat
看看	to take a look
请你试试这双球鞋。	Please try this pair of sneakers.
我能看看你的书吗？	Can I take a look at your book?

6. 从……V. 到…… (from … to …)

This pattern can be used to express the duration of an action, spatial distance, or the range of topics an action covers.

▶ 我们从家里的事情谈到学习的事情。
We talk about topics ranging from family to study.

他从昨天晚上八点睡到今天上午十点。
He slept from eight last night to ten this morning.

7. 对somebody来说 (for somebody, as far as somebody is concerned)

▶ 学英文对中国人来说很难。
Learning English is very hard for Chinese people.

早上9点上课对我来说太早了！
To have class at 9 a.m. is too early for me!

8. 千万

千万 is used only in imperative sentences to emphasize that somebody must or must not do something. It is often used in negative sentences followed by 别, 不要, 不能. When used in an affirmative sentence, it is often followed by 得 or 要.

▶ 在饭馆儿里，千万不能把"水饺"说成"睡觉"。
In a restaurant, be sure not to pronounce "shuǐjiǎo" as "shuìjiào."

上课的时候千万别睡觉。
Be sure not to sleep in class.

明天考试，你们千万要早点儿来。
There is an exam tomorrow. Be sure to arrive earlier.

9. Complement 成

成 in this text means "as," often used in this pattern:

把 A + V. (说/写/看/听) + 成 + B

The pattern sometimes indicates that a mistake has been made or that the actual situation is not the same as is presented.

▶ 他把"水饺"说成"睡觉"，闹了个大笑话。
He pronounced "shuǐjiǎo" as "shuìjiào," and made a big fool of himself.

考试的时候我把"大"写成了"太"。
In the exam, I miswrote 大 as 太.

個別談話

　　老師們為了讓大家有練習說中文的機會，安排每個同學每兩個星期和老師見一次面。見面的時候，可以談談上課的時候不能談的話題。我們把這個活動叫做"個別談話"。我最喜歡個別談話，因為個別談話很輕鬆，學到的東西也很多。

　　我和王老師最談得來。上課的時候，我們是老師和學生，個別談話的時候，我們是好朋友。我們從家裏的事情談到學習的事情，從學中文談到學英文。以前我覺得英文很容易，和王老師談話以後才發現，學英文對中國人來說很難。

　　老師們都很注意我們的發音。中文的發音很難，但是也很重要。要是發音不對，就會鬧很大的笑話。在飯館兒裏，千萬不能把"水餃"說成"睡覺"。要是一個男學生問一個女服務員的時候，把"水餃一碗多少錢？"說成"睡覺一晚多少錢？"他可能會有很大的麻煩。

　　每次個別談話只有15分鐘，我覺得太短了。但是，對老師來說，15分鐘並不短，因為他們每個星期都得跟很多學生談話。

24 Kàn Diànyǐng (See a Movie)

Pinyin Text

(A—Xiǎoyīng, B—Zhāng Sān)

A: Zuótiān wǎnshàng, wǒ zài xuéxiào de diànyǐngyuàn kànle yíge Zhōngguó diànyǐng, hǎokàn jíle, nǐ kànle ma?

B: Wǒ méikàn. Yǐqián nǐ kànguo Zhōngguó diànyǐng ma?

A: Méi kànguo, zhè shì wǒ dìyīcì kàn Zhōngguó diànyǐng.

B: Nǐ kàndǒngle ma?

A: Méiyǒu quán kàndǒng, kěshì zhīdào diànyǐng de gùshi.

B: Shì shénme gùshi ne?

English Translation

(A—Xiaoying, B—Zhang San)

A: Last night, I saw a Chinese movie in the school theater. It's very good. Did you see it?

B: I didn't. Had you seen Chinese movies before?

A: No, I hadn't. That was the first time I went to see a Chinese movie.

B: Did you understand it?

A: Not entirely, but I know the story of the movie.

B: What's the story?

第二十四课 看电影

(A——小英，B——张三)

A: 昨天晚上，我在学校的电影院看了一个中国电影，好看极了，你看了吗？

B: 我没看。以前你看过中国电影吗？

A: 没看过，这是我第一次看中国电影。

B: 你看懂了吗？

A: 没有全看懂，可是知道电影的故事。

B: 是什么故事呢？

电影	電影	diànyǐng	n.	movie
电影院	電影院	diànyǐng yuàn	n.	movie theater, cinema
好看		hǎokàn	adj.	interesting (for books, movies, TV programs, etc.)
全		quán	adj./adv.	entire; completely, entirely
故事		gùshi	n.	story

A: Shì ge àiqíng gùshi. Hěnduō nián yǐqián, zài Běijīng yǒu yíge hěn piàoliang de gū'niang hé yíge xiǎohuǒzi tán liàn'ài. Gū'niang hěn'ài nèige xiǎohuǒzi, yòu gěitā zuòfàn, yòu gěitā xǐ yīfu. Kěshì xiǎohuǒzi bìng búài nèigè gū'niang, tā háiyǒu biéde nǚ péngyou. Hòulái, tā gēn biérén jiéhūn le. Nèige gū'niang chībúxià fàn, yě shuìbuzháo jiào, zuìhòu bìngsǐle.

B: Zhè shì yíge ràng rén hěn nánguò de gùshi, nǐ zěnme shuō hǎokàn jíle ne?

A: It is a love story. Many years ago, there was a very pretty girl in Beijing dating a young man. The girl loved the young man very much: she cooked and washed clothes for him. However that young man didn't love the girl. He had other girlfriends. Later, he married someone else. The girl could neither eat nor sleep. In the end, she died from illness.

B: This is a story that makes people sad. How can you say it is very good?

爱情	爱情	àiqíng	n.	romantic love
年		nián	n.	year
姑娘		gū'niang	n.	girl, young woman
小伙子		xiǎohuǒzi	n.	lad, young man
谈恋爱	談戀愛	tánliàn'ài	phrase	to date, to be in love
爱	愛	ài	v./n.	to love; love
做饭	做飯	zuòfàn	v.o.	to cook food
洗		xǐ	v.	to wash
吃不下		chībúxià	v.c.	cannot swallow
最后	最後	zuìhòu	conj.	in the end
病		bìng	v.	to get sick
难过	難過	nánguò	adj.	sad

A: 是个爱情故事。很多年以前，在北京有一个很漂亮的姑娘和一个小伙子谈恋爱。姑娘很爱那个小伙子，又给他做饭，又给他洗衣服。可是小伙子并不爱那个姑娘，他还有别的女朋友。后来，他跟别人结婚了。那个姑娘吃不下饭，也睡不着觉，最后病死了。

B: 这是一个让人很难过的故事，你怎么说好看极了呢？

Anne Karelnikov

A: Wǒ jiùshì ài kàn ràng rén nánguò de diànyǐng. Zuótiān wǒ yìbiān kàn, yìbiān kū. Zhèige diànyǐng ràng wǒ xiǎngqǐ le yǐqián de nán péngyou, tā jiùxiàng diànyǐng lǐ de nèige rén yíyàng, yìbiān gēn wǒ tán liàn'ài, yìbiān yòu gēn biérén tán liàn'ài. Dào xiànzài wǒ hái hèntā ne! Hǎoxiàng nánrén dōu shì zhèyàng.

B: Zhèige wǒ bù tóngyì. Qíshí nǚrén yěshì zhèyàng. Wǒ yǐqián de nǚ péngyou hé wǒ tán liàn'ài de shíhou, háiyǒu biéde nán péngyou. Yǒushíhou, tā yìbiān hé wǒ hē kāfēi hái yìbiān yòng shǒujī hé lìng yíge nán péngyou liáotiānr ne!

A: Nǐde nèigè nǚpéngyou zhēn shì ge huàidàn! Xiàcì wǒ qǐng nǐ kàn diànyǐng.

B: Hǎo jíle! Nǐ qǐng wǒ kàn diànyǐng, wǒ qǐng nǐ chīfàn.

A: I like movies that make people sad. Yesterday, while I was watching the movie, I cried along. This movie made me think of my ex-boyfriend. He is just like the man in the movie. While he was dating me, he was also dating others. I have been hating him ever since! It seems men are all like this.

B: I don't agree with you on this. In fact, women are also like this. When my ex-girlfriend was dating me, she also had other boyfriends. Sometimes, she talked with another boyfriend on her cell phone while having coffee with me!

A: That ex-girlfriend of yours really is a rotten egg! Next time I'll treat you to a movie.

B: Great! You treat me to a movie, and I'll treat you to dinner.

哭		kū	v.	to cry, to weep
想起		xiǎngqǐ	v.c.	to think of (suddenly)
像……一样	一样	xiàng … yíyàng	prep.	be like, as
恨		hèn	v.	to hate

A: 我就是爱看让人难过的电影。昨天我一边看，一边哭。这个电影让我想起了以前的男朋友，他就像电影里的那个人一样，一边跟我谈恋爱，一边又跟别人谈恋爱。到现在我还恨他呢！好像男人都是这样。

B: 这个我不同意。其实女人也是这样。我以前的女朋友和我谈恋爱的时候还有别的男朋友。 有时候， 她一边和我喝咖啡还一边用手机和另一个男朋友聊天儿呢！

A: 你的那个女朋友真是个坏蛋！下次我请你看电影。

B: 好极了！你请我看电影，我请你吃饭。

男人		nánrén	n.	man, male
同意		tóngyì	v.	to agree
女人		nǚrén	n.	woman, female
坏蛋	壞蛋	huàidàn	n.	a rotten egg, a bad person

语法 Grammar Notes

1. Review: Verb Suffix 过

过 used as a verb suffix means "to have had the experience" in the past. For a detailed explanation, see grammar note 2 in Lesson 4.

▶ 你以前看过中国电影没有？
Have you seen Chinese movies before?

没看过。
I haven't.

你吃过中国饭没有？
Have you had Chinese food before?

吃过很多次。
I've had it many times.

2. Review: 以前

以前 may stand by itself as a time word, meaning "before, in the past."

你以前谈过恋爱没有？
Have you dated anyone before?

以前 can be appended to a time word or an action or an event to indicate "before" that referential point.

▶ 结婚以前，他谈过几次恋爱。
He dated several times before he got married.

以前 can be appended to an expression of time duration to indicate some time ago.

▶ 很多年以前，在北京有一个很漂亮的姑娘和一个小伙子谈恋爱。
Many years ago, there was a very pretty girl in Beijing dating a young man.

3. 全 (entirely, totally)

Like the adverb 都, 全 is another word that marks the all-inclusiveness of the action. 全 is more emphatic in connotation than 都, and the two can be combined to further enhance the idea of totality.

▶ 这个电影我没有全看懂。
I didn't totally understand this movie.

我的家人全 (都) 来学校了。
My family all came to the school.

4. 后来 (later, later on) vs. 最后 (at last; in the end)

后来 always refers to events in the past.

▶ 后来他跟别人结婚了。
Later, he married another person.

最后 describes the last of a series of actions or events.

▶ 最后那个姑娘病死了。
In the end, that girl died from illness.

美国人吃饭的时候，先喝汤，再吃菜，最后吃甜点。
When Americans have meals, they have soup first, then the dishes, and eat dessert last.

5. 同意 (to agree)

同意 is used to confirm one's agreement. When you agree with someone, you can either say 我同意 or 我同意你的看法.

▶ 这个我同意。
I agree (with you) on this.

6. Review: 用 + Instrument + Verb

用 in this pattern is often translated into "using" or "with." Because it is a first position verb, to negate the sentence, 不 is placed before 用, not before the main verb.

▶ 她用手机跟另一个男朋友聊天儿。
She used her cell phone to chat with another boyfriend.

我们用笔写字。
We write with a pen.

7. 跟/和 + Somebody + V.P.

The prepositions 跟 and 和, both of which mean "and, with," are naturally used to translate English phrases that share a similar structure as their Chinese counterparts. For example, "to talk with the teacher" is "跟老师谈话" in Chinese; "to go to New York with you" is "和你去纽约." In both examples, "with" is directly rendered as 跟 or 和. However, there are some phrases in English that do not have "with," but when they are translated into Chinese, the structure "跟/和 + somebody + V.P." has to be used. The following three examples are all about human relationships.

To meet somebody	跟 somebody 见面
To date somebody	跟 somebody 谈恋爱
To marry somebody	跟 somebody 结婚

Traditional Character Text

看電影

(A——小英，B——張三)

A: 昨天晚上，我在學校的電影院看了一個中國電影，好看極了，你看了嗎？

B: 我沒看。以前你看過中國電影嗎？

A: 沒看過，這是我第一次看中國電影。

B: 你看懂了嗎？

A: 沒有全看懂，可是知道電影的故事。

B: 是什麼故事呢？

A: 是個愛情故事。很多年以前，在北京有一個很漂亮的姑娘和一個小伙子談戀愛。姑娘很愛那個小伙子，又給他做飯，又給他洗衣服。可是小伙子並不愛那個姑娘，他還有別的女朋友。後來，他跟別人結婚了。那個姑娘吃不下飯，也睡不著覺，最後病死了。

B: 這是一個讓人很難過的故事，你怎麼說好看極了呢？

A: 我就是愛看讓人難過的電影，昨天我一邊看，一邊哭。這個電影讓我想起了以前的男朋友，他就像電影裏的那個人一樣，一邊跟我談戀愛，一邊又跟別人談戀愛。到現在我還恨他呢！好像男人都是這樣。

B: 這個我不同意。其實女人也是這樣。我以前的女朋友和我談
戀愛的時候還有別的男朋友。有時候，她一邊和我喝咖啡還
一邊用手機和另一個男朋友聊天兒呢！

A: 你的那個女朋友真是個壞蛋！下次我請你看電影。

B: 好極了！你請我看電影，我請你吃飯。

25 Wǒ Chīsù (I'm Vegetarian)

Pinyin Text

(A—Xiǎoyīng, B—Zhāng Sān)

A: Xiǎo Zhāng, jīntiān de niúròu hěn hǎochī, nǐ zěnme yìdiǎnr dōu bùchī ne?

B: Wǒ yǐqián yě hěn xǐhuān chī niúròu, xiànzài bùchī le. Yīshēng shuō chīròu duì shēntǐ bùhǎo, wǒ cóng liǎngnián qián jiù kāishǐ chīsù le.

A: Wǒ juéde yīshēng shuō de huà yě bùyídìng dōu duì. Wǒ yéye jiù xǐhuān chīròu, měitiān búshì chī niúròu, jiùshì chī zhūròu, xiànzài dōu kuài jiǔshí suì le, shēntǐ hái hěn jiànkāng ne. Wǒ shūshu, yòu bùchī niúròu, yòu bùchī zhūròu, lián yú hé jīdàn dōu bùgǎn chī, měitiān zhǐ chī qīngcài, búdào liùshí suì jiù sǐ le. Suǒyǐ wǒ juéde, chī shénme gēn jiànkāng bù yídìng yǒu guānxi, zuì zhòngyào de shì duànliàn.

English Translation

(A—Xiaoying, B—Zhang San)

A: Little Zhang, today's beef is delicious. How come you didn't eat any of it at all?

B: Before, I used to like beef very much, but now I don't eat it. The doctor said that eating meat was not good for my health. I became a vegetarian two years ago.

A: I don't think that what doctors say is always right. My grandfather likes to eat meat. Every day, if he doesn't eat beef, he eats pork. Now he is almost ninety years old and is still very healthy. My uncle ate neither beef nor pork. He didn't even dare to eat fish or eggs. He ate only vegetables every day, but he died before he reached sixty. Therefore, I think what you eat is not necessarily related to your health. The most important thing is to exercise.

吃素		chīsù	v.	to eat vegetables, to be vegetarian
医生	醫生	yīshēng	n.	doctor
开始		kāishǐ	v.	to start, to begin

第二十五课 我吃素

（A——小英，B——张三）

A：小张，今天的牛肉很好吃，你怎么一点儿都不吃呢？

B：我以前也很喜欢吃牛肉，现在不吃了。医生说吃肉对身体不好，我从两年前就开始吃素了。

A：我觉得医生说的话也不一定都对。我爷爷就喜欢吃肉，每天不是吃牛肉，就是吃猪肉，现在都快90岁了，身体还很健康呢。我叔叔又不吃牛肉，又不吃猪肉，连鱼和鸡蛋都不敢吃，每天只吃青菜，不到60岁就死了。所以我觉得，吃什么跟健康不一定有关系，最重要的是锻炼。

(不)一定		(bù)yídìng	adv.	(not) necessarily, (not) certainly
爷爷	爺爺	yéye	n.	grandfather (paternal)
快		kuài	adv.	nearly
身体	身體	shēntǐ	n.	body, health
叔叔		shūshu	n.	uncle
鸡蛋		jīdàn	n.	egg
敢		gǎn	v.	dare (to do something)
关系	關係	guānxì	n.	relationship

B: Zhèige wǒ bù tóngyì. Wǒ nǎinai jīnnián jiǔshíwǔ suì le, cónglái dōu bú yùndòng, lián qù línjū jiā dōu kāichē, kěshì tā cónglái méi shēngguobìng. Wǒ ā'yí jīnnián cái sìshí wǔ suì, měitiān búshì pǎobù, jiùshì dǎ wǎngqiú. Shàngge yuè qù yīyuàn jiǎnchá, yīshēng shuō tā yǒu xīnzàng bìng.

A: Tīng nǐ zhème shuō, hǎoxiàng zuò shénme gēn jiànkāng dōu méiyǒu guānxi. Nándào wǒmen shénme dōu búzuò, shēntǐ jiù huì hěn jiànkāng ma?

B: Yíge rén shēntǐ hǎobuhǎo, chī shénme, zuò shénme, dōu bú zhòngyào, zuì zhòngyào de shì yǒuméiyǒu jiànkāng de fùmǔ. Fùmǔ jiànkāng, háizi dàduō yě jiànkāng; fùmǔ yǒubìng, háizi yě chángcháng huì yǒu yíyàng de bìng.

A: Suǒyǐ, yǒuqián de fùmǔ bùrú jiànkāng de fùmǔ.

B: I don't agree with you on this. My grandmother is ninety-five years old this year. She never exercises. Even when she goes to her neighbor's house, she drives. However, she has never gotten sick. My aunt is only forty-five years old this year. Every day, if she doesn't run, she plays tennis. Last month, she went to the hospital to have a physical examination. The doctor said that she had heart disease.

A: From what you said, it seems that what we do is not related to our health at all. Shall we not do anything and expect that our body will be healthy?

B: It doesn't matter what one eats or what one does. The most important factor in whether a person's health is good or not is the health of his parents. If parents are healthy, their children are mostly healthy. If parents are sick, their children will often have the same disease.

A: Therefore, wealthy parents are not as good as healthy parents.

奶奶		nǎinai	n.	grandmother (paternal)
今年		jīnnián	n.	this year
邻居	鄰居	línjū	n.	neighbor

B：这个我不同意。我奶奶今年95岁了，从来都不运动，连去邻居家都开车，可是她从来没生过病。我阿姨今年才45岁，每天不是跑步，就是打网球。上个月去医院检查，医生说她有心脏病。

A：听你这么说，好像做什么跟健康都没有关系。难道我们什么都不做，身体就会很健康吗？

B：一个人身体好不好，吃什么，做什么，都不重要，最重要的是他有没有健康的父母。父母健康，孩子大多也健康；父母有病，孩子也常常会有一样的病。

A：所以，有钱的父母不如健康的父母。

阿姨		ā'yí	n.	aunt
才		cái	adv.	only
检查	檢查	jiǎnchá	v.	to check, to examine
心脏病	心臟病	xīnzàngbìng	n.	heart disease
父母		fùmǔ	n.	father and mother, parents
不如		bùrú	prep.	not as good as, not as … as

语法 Grammar Notes

1. A对 B 好/不好 (A is good/not good for B)

In this structure, "A" and "B" are very flexible, and they can be noun phrases or verb phrases.

▶ 医生说吃肉对身体不好。

The doctor said that eating meat was not good for my health.

总是看电脑对眼睛不好。

Looking at the computer (screen) for too long is not good for the eyes.

2. Review: 又 Adj.1/V.1，又 Adj.2/V.2 (both … and …)

This is an emphatic pattern to express "both … and. …" 又 is an adverb, thus it must precede an adjective or verb, never a noun.

▶ 我叔叔又不吃牛肉，又不吃猪肉。

My uncle eats neither beef nor pork.

他的新朋友又高又瘦。

His new friend is both tall and thin.

3. 才 (only)

We learned in Lesson 14 that 才 is used as an adverb to indicate that an action appears later than expected. It is often translated as "not … until. …"

我今天早上10点才起来。

I didn't get up until ten this morning.

In this lesson, 才 means "only" in the structure 才 + **amount**.

▶ 我阿姨今年才45岁。

My aunt is only 45 years old this year.

这双鞋才30块钱。

This pair of shoes is only 30 dollars.

4. A 跟 B (是) 没有关系(的) (A has nothing to do with B)

This pattern expresses that two incidents have nothing to do with each other. The incidents "A" and "B" are often in question forms, as demonstrated in the examples below. "是……的" can be added for emphasis. The opposite meaning of this pattern would be "A跟B 有(很大的)关系".

▶ 吃什么跟健康不一定有关系，最重要的是锻炼。
What you eat is not necessarily related to your health. The most important thing is to exercise.

有时候做什么工作跟专业并没有关系。
Sometimes what job one is doing is actually not related to his major.

Compare this to the grammar note on "……没有关系，重要的是……" in Lesson 15. 没有关系 in this case means "doesn't matter," and it often appears in the negative form.

5. 不如 (not as ... as)

不如 is used in comparison, there are two basic sentence patterns:

(1) A 不如 B

B is higher or better than A in the aspect in which they are compared. A and B can be nouns, verbs, or clauses, but usually they have similar or symmetrical structures.

▶ 有钱的父母不如健康的父母。
Wealthy parents are not as good as healthy parents.

开车不如走路。
Driving is not as good as walking.

(2) A 不如 B + adj./verb + complement

The additional information provided by the adjective or the verb complement is to specify the aspect in which A and B are compared.

在纽约，有时候开车不如走路快。
In New York, sometimes driving is not as fast as walking.

跑步不如打网球有意思。
Running is not as interesting as playing tennis.

Cultural Notes

Chinese People's New Concept of a Healthy Lifestyle

"Chicken, duck, fish, and pork" (鸡鸭鱼肉 , jī yā yú ròu), a term that symbolized a wealthy and good life in the 1980s and 1990s in China, is now completely out of fashion, and even considered a very unhealthy diet. Chinese people now realize that eating too much meat may give rise to obesity and other serious health problems. To maintain a balanced diet, eating more vegetables and less meat is now widely accepted by Chinese. In big cities, vegetarian restaurants have become popular and proved to be profitable. To help satisfy the wishes of many customers to stay away from meat but still enjoy the taste of it, vegetarian restaurants have created dishes made from 豆腐 (dòufu, tofu) and 青菜 (qīngcài, green vegetables) that look and taste like meat. If you get a chance to visit the Shaolin Buddhist Temple in Henan province someday, don't forget to try their vegetarian feast. It is renowned as quite delicious.

Along with the fashion of a more balanced diet, doing more exercise and practicing the traditional Chinese way of cultivating good health are hot topics in China today. You will hear sayings such as "请朋友吃饭不如请朋友锻炼" (inviting friends to eat is not as good as inviting them to exercise), and you will see in bookstores numerous newly published books on traditional Chinese methods to cultivate "气" (qì, spiritual energy) through special food therapies.

Traditional Character Text

我吃素

(A——小英，B——張三)

A：小張，今天的牛肉很好吃，你怎麼一點兒都不吃呢？

B：我以前也很喜歡吃牛肉，現在不吃了。醫生說吃肉對身體不好，我從兩年前就開始吃素了。

A：我覺得醫生說的話也不一定都對。我爺爺就喜歡吃肉，每天不是吃牛肉，就是吃豬肉，現在都快90歲了，身體還很健康呢。我叔叔又不吃牛肉，又不吃豬肉，連魚和雞蛋都不敢吃，每天只吃青菜，不到60歲就死了。所以我覺得，吃什麼跟健康不一定有關係，最重要的是鍛煉。

B：這個我不同意。我奶奶今年95歲了，從來都不運動，連去鄰居家都開車，可是她從來沒生過病。我阿姨今年才45歲，每天不是跑步，就是打網球。上個月去醫院檢查，醫生說她有心臟病。

A：聽你這麼說，好像做什麼跟健康都沒有關係。難道我們什麼都不做，身體就會很健康嗎？

B：一個人身體好不好，吃什麼，做什麼，都不重要，最重要的是他有沒有健康的父母。父母健康，孩子大多也健康；父母有病，孩子也常常會有一樣的病。

A：所以，有錢的父母不如健康的父母。

Yǎnjiǎng Bǐsài
(Speech Contest)

Pinyin Text

Měinián wǔyuè, chūnjì xuéqī kuài jiéshù de shíhou, wèile ràng xué Zhōngwén de xuéshēng liànxí shuōhuà, Dōngyà xì dōu huì jǔbàn yícì Zhōngwén yǎnjiǎng bǐsài. Jīnnián cānjiā de xuéshēng hěnduō, yóuqí shì yī niánjí de xuéshēng, chàbuduō yǒu sānshí ge rén. Bǐsài yǐqián, xuéshēng xiān xiě yìpiān wénzhāng, ràng lǎoshī gǎizhèng yǐhòu zài liànxí. Wáng lǎoshī hái bāng wǒ zuòle lùyīn, wǒ tīng le hěnduō cì, gēnzhe niàn, zuìhòu, wǒ bǎ wénzhāng dōu bèi xiàlái le.

Běnlái wǒ bùxiǎng cānjiā, yīnwèi zài hěnduō rén miànqián shuōhuà, ràng wǒ hěn jǐnzhāng. Shàngcì wǒ cānjiā le yíge Yīngwén yǎnjiǎng bǐsài, wǒ jǐnzhāng de shuōbuchū huà lái. Kěshì zhèicì yòng Zhōngwén yǎnjiǎng, wǒ què bú nàme jǐnzhāng le.

English Translation

Every year in May when the spring semester is about to end, in order to make students of Chinese practice speaking the language, the Department of East Asian Studies will organize a Chinese speech contest. The students who participated in the contest this year were numerous, especially the first-year students, of which there were about thirty. Before the contest, the students would first write an essay, ask the teacher to correct it, and then practice. Teacher Wang also helped me to make a recording. I listened to it many times and read along with it. Finally, I memorized the essay.

Originally, I did not want to participate [in the contest], because speaking in front of many people makes me very nervous. Last time I took part in an English speech contest, I was so nervous that I could not say a word. However, this time I made my speech in Chinese, I was not that nervous.

第二十六课 演讲比赛

　　每年五月，春季学期快结束的时候，为了让学中文的学生练习说话，东亚系都会举办一次中文演讲比赛。今年参加的学生很多，尤其是一年级的学生，差不多有30个人。比赛以前，学生先写一篇文章，让老师改正以后再练习。王老师还帮我做了录音，我听了很多次，跟着念，最后，我把文章都背下来了。

　　本来我不想参加，因为在很多人面前说话，让我很紧张。上次我参加了一个英文演讲比赛，我紧张得说不出话来。可是这次用中文演讲，我却不那么紧张了。

演讲	演講	yǎnjiǎng	v./n.	to deliver a speech; speech
比赛	比賽	bǐsài	n.	competition
每年		měinián	n.	every year
春季		chūnjì	n.	spring
结束	結束	jiéshù	v.	to end
举办	舉辦	jǔbàn	v.	to organize (an event)
参加	參加	cānjiā	v.	to take part in, to participate
尤其		yóuqí	adv.	especially
篇		piān	m.w.	measure word for articles, essays
文章		wénzhāng	n.	article, essay
改正		gǎizhèng	v.	to correct
跟着	跟著	gēnzhe	v.	to follow
念		niàn	v.	to read (aloud)
本来	本來	běnlái	adv.	originally
在 somebody 面前		zài … miànqián	prep.	in the face of … , in front of …
却	卻	què	adv.	but, yet

Zhèicì bǐsài yǒu yī niánjí de tóngxué, yěyǒu sān sì niánjí de tóngxué. Yī niánjí tóngxué shuō de huà, wǒ dōu tīngdedǒng; dànshì sān sì niánjí tóngxué shuō de huà, wǒ jiù tīng bú tài dǒng le. Wúlùn wǒ tīngdǒng le méiyǒu, wǒ dōu juéde fēicháng yǒu yìsi.

Yǎnjiǎng bǐsài jiéshù yǐhòu, Zhōu lǎoshī gēn dàjiā shuō le huà, tāshuō: "cānjiā bǐsài, shūyíng méiyǒu guānxi, zuì zhòngyào de shì liànxí shuō Zhōngwén." Zhèige kànfǎ wǒ bù wánquán tóngyì. Jìrán cānjiā le bǐsài, wǒ dāngrán jiù xīwàng yíng. Dànshì hòulái wǒ fāxiàn, dìyī míng de jiǎngjīn cái wǔshí kuài qián, wǒ xiǎng, Zhōu lǎoshī de huà qíshí shì duìde.

In this contest, there were first-year students and third-year and fourth-year students as well. As for what the first-year students said, I could understand it all; however, as for what the third-year and fourth-year students said, I could not really understand it. No matter whether I understood it or not, I found it very interesting.

After the speech contest, Teacher Zhou talked to everyone. He said, "When one participates in a contest, winning or losing does not matter. The most important thing is to practice speaking Chinese." I do not totally agree with this opinion. Given the fact that I already participated in the contest, I of course hoped to win. However, later I found out that the prize for the first place winner was only fifty dollars. I think that Teacher Zhou's words were actually correct.

输	輸	shū	v.	to lose
赢	贏	yíng	v.	to win
当然		dāngrán	adv.	of course, certainly
第一名		dìyīmíng	phrase	the first place
奖金	獎金	jiǎngjīn	n.	prize; bonus

这次比赛有一年级的同学，也有三、四年级的同学。一年级同学说的话，我都听得懂；但是三、四年级同学说的话，我就听不太懂了。无论我听懂了没有，我都觉得非常有意思。

演讲比赛结束以后，周老师跟大家说了话。他说："参加比赛，输赢没关系，最重要的是练习说中文。"这个看法我不完全同意。既然参加了比赛，我当然就希望赢。但是后来我发现，第一名的奖金才50块钱，我想，周老师的话其实是对的。

语法 Grammar Notes

1. Review 每 + Measure Word + Noun (every)

Some time words, such as 天 and 年, can serve as measure words themselves; therefore no additional measure word is needed after 每. Consider, for example, every day 每天 and every year 每年. The following table shows whether a measure word is required with some common time words to express "every. ..."

every	分 minute	小时 hour	天 day	星期 week	月 month	年 year	学期 semester
每	✓	✓	✓	✓	✓	✓	✓
每个	N/A	✓	N/A	✓	✓	N/A	✓

In English, "every noun" is treated as a singular concept; however, in Chinese, it is a collective concept. Therefore, phrases with 每 are usually followed by 都.

▶ 每年五月，东亚系都会举办一次中文演讲比赛。

Every year in May, the Department of East Asian Studies will organize a Chinese speech contest.

他每个学期都有中文课。

He has Chinese class every semester.

2. 快V.P.的时候 (when ... is about to. ...)

快 as an adjective means "fast, quick." Here it is used as an adverb, indicating an pending situation, that is, something is about to happen.

▶ 春季学期快结束的时候

When the spring semester is about to end

快考试的时候，学生们都很忙。

When the examination is getting close, students are all very busy.

3. Review 为了 + V.P./N.P. (in order to do … /for the purpose of …)

The subject of the sentence can be placed either at the very beginning, that is, before 为了, or at the beginning of the second clause after the purpose has been stated.

▶ 为了让学生练习说话，东亚系每年都会举办中文演讲比赛。

In order to make students practice speaking Chinese, the Department of East Asian Studies will organize a Chinese speech contest every year.

为了准备考试，他昨天晚上没有睡觉。

In order to prepare for the examination, he didn't sleep last night.

4. 举办 + Activities (to organize activities)

The most often seen phrases with 举办 include the following ones:

举办比赛	to organize a competition
举办活动	to organize an activity
举办晚会 (wǎnhuì, party)	to organize a party

5. 尤其 (especially)

尤其 is used when all members of a group are outstanding in some respect, but one or more are picked out to be especially outstanding. It often appears at the beginning of the second clause of a sentence. 尤其 is used in the following patterns:

尤其 + adj.

……，尤其是 + noun phrase/prepositional phrase (to be put at the beginning of the second clause)

▶ 今年参加的学生很多，尤其是一年级的学生。

Students who participated [in the contest] this year are numerous, especially the first-year students.

中国的东西很便宜，尤其是衣服。

Things in China are inexpensive, especially clothes.

The same sentence above can be translated in another way, as follows:

中国的东西很便宜，衣服尤其便宜。

6. 让 (to let; to make)

让 as a verb has two major functions.

(1) A 让 B V.P.: A ask/let B (to) do something

▶ 学生让老师改正文章。

The students asked the teacher to correct their essays.

学校不让学生在图书馆打电话。

The school doesn't allow students to make calls in the library.

(2) Some situation causes certain effects

Topic (which can be a simple word, a phrase, or a longer clause) 让 somebody V.P.

▶ 在很多人面前说话，让我很紧张。

Speaking in front of many people makes me very nervous.

每天在图书馆看书让他觉得很累。

Reading books in the library every day makes him feel very tired.

7. ......, (但是/可是/不过) subject 却 V.P. (... , but subject V.P.)

The adverb 却, which comes after the subject, is often paired with 但是/可是/不过 to emphasize the tone of contrast.

▶ 可是这次用中文演讲，我却不那么紧张了。

However, this time I made my speech in Chinese, I was not that nervous.

我的朋友都喜欢在图书馆看书，我却喜欢在宿舍看书。

All my friends like to read in the library, but I actually like to read in my dorm room.

8. 先 V.P.1, V.P.2 以后再 V.P.3, 最后 V.P.4 (first V.P.1, after V.P.2, then V.P.3, finally V.P.4)

This structure is used to describe a series of actions. A variance of this pattern is 先 V.P.1, 然后 V.P.2, 再 V.P.3, 最后 V.P.4, which means first ... , then ... , then ... , and finally. ... It doesn't have to be four actions in a row. One may just keep one of the middle two parts, that is, either use 然后, or 再, and does not have to include both.

▶ 学生先写一篇文章，让老师改正以后再练习。

The student would write an essay first, ask the teacher to correct it, and then practice.

学中文的时候，你应该先听录音，然后练习写中国字。

When studying Chinese, you should first listen to the recordings, and then practice writing characters.

9. 跟着 (somebody/something) V.P. (to follow somebody or something to do …)

▶ 我跟着（录音）念。   I read (the essay) following (the recording).

学生跟着老师学中文。   The students study Chinese with the teacher.

10. Adj. 得 + Complement

This structure indicates the degree or extent of the adjective. The complement after 得 can be a simple word or a compound phrase .

▶ 我紧张得说不出话来。   I was so nervous that I could not speak.

他高兴得跳了起来。   He was so happy that he jumped up.

In the first example, 出(out) is used as the complement. 说不出话来 is the negative potential form of the verb phrase. The positive potential form 说得出话来 is only used in a limited number of special circumstances.

Another often used verb to take 出 as a complement is 写. For example,

这个字，你写得出来写不出来？

Can you write (out) this character?

11. Review 无论……, Subject 都 V.P. (not matter/regardless of …)

The clause that follows 无论 must be one of the following three types:

(1) Clause with a question word, such as what, who, why, when, where, how, and how many; in Chinese 什么，谁，为什么，什么时候/几点, 哪儿，怎么，多少/几。

无论你想去哪儿，我都跟你一起去。

No matter where you want to go, I will go with you.

(2) Yes/no question

▶ 无论我听懂了没有，我都觉得非常有意思。

No matter whether I understood it or not, I thought it very interesting.

无论你明年去不去中国，你都应该开始学中文。

No matter whether you will go to China or not next year, you should start to learn Chinese.

(3) Selective question: 无论(是)A 还是B, Subject 都V.P.

无论是中国饭还是美国饭，他都喜欢吃。

No matter whether it is Chinese food or American food, he likes to eat it.

12. Review 既然……, Subject 就…… (given the fact that/it being the case that ... , then ...)

This sentence structure always starts with 既然, and the second clause can be one with 就, which means "then" in this case, or it can be a question.

▶ 既然参加了比赛，我当然就希望赢。
Given the fact that I already participated in the contest, I of course wanted to win.

既然你很喜欢吃中国饭，为什么你不会用筷子？
Given the fact that you like to eat Chinese food, how come you can't use chopsticks?

13. Review 才 (only; not ... until)

才, an adverb, has various meanings. In this text, it means "only," similar to 只 or 只有, and it is always followed by number or amount.

▶ 第一名的奖金才80块钱。
The prize for the first place winner was only eighty dollars.

他才16岁，还不能喝酒。
He is only sixteen years old and he can't drink yet.

The other main meaning of 才 is to indicate that an action happens later than what the speaker expected. It is often translated as "not ... until," with the order of the clause reversed in English.

我叔叔60岁才开始锻炼身体。
My uncle didn't start to exercise until he was sixty years old.

我明天下午才有时间。
I won't have time until tomorrow afternoon.

Traditional Character Text

演講比賽

　　每年五月，春季學期快結束的時候，爲了讓學中文的學生練習說話，東亞系都會舉辦一次中文演講比賽。今年參加的學生很多，尤其是一年級的學生，差不多有30個人。比賽以前，學生先寫一篇文章，讓老師改正以後再練習。王老師還幫我做了錄音。我聽了很多次，跟著念，最後，我把文章都背下來了。

　　本來我不想參加，因爲在很多人面前說話，讓我很緊張。上次我參加了一個英文演講比賽，我緊張得說不出話來。可是這次用中文演講，我卻不那麼緊張了。

　　這次比賽有一年級的同學，也有三、四年級的同學。一年級同學說的話，我都聽得懂；但是三、四年級同學說的話，我就聽不太懂了。無論我聽懂了沒有，我都覺得非常有意思。

　　演講比賽結束以後，周老師跟大家說了話。他說："參加比賽，輸贏沒關係，最重要的是練習說中文。"這個看法我不完全同意。既然參加了比賽，我當然就希望贏。但是後來我發現，第一名的獎金才50塊錢。我想，周老師的話其實是對的。

27 Wǒ Děi Bānjiā (I Have to Move)

Pinyin Text

(A—Xiǎoyīng, B—Māma)

A: Mā, zhù zài sùshè lǐ tài bù fāngbiàn le, wǒ xiǎng bān dào xiàowài qù zhù.

B: Sùshè lí jiàoshì hé túshūguǎn dōu hěnjìn, nǐ zěnme shuō bù fāngbiàn ne?

A: Fángjiān lǐ méiyǒu cèsuǒ, yě méiyǒu yùshì, měitiān zǎoshàng dōu děi děng bàntiān cáinéng xǐzǎo. Wǒ chángcháng chídào, jiùshì yīnwèi yòng cèsuǒ de rén tàiduōle.

B: Nà nǐ zǎodiǎnr qǐlái, jiù búyòng děng le.

A: Wǒ měitiān zuò zuòyè zuò dào yì liǎng diǎn cái shuìjiào, zǎoshàng gēnběn qǐbulái.

English Translation

(A—Xiaoying, B—Mother)

A: Mom, living in the dorm is too inconvenient. I want to move off campus.

B: The dorm is close to both your classrooms and the library. How can you say it is inconvenient?

A: There is no restroom or shower in my room. I have to wait for ages to take a shower every morning. The reason that I am often late for classes is that there are too many people using the bathroom.

B: In that case, if you got up earlier, you wouldn't have to wait.

A: I do my homework and don't sleep until one or two every day. I can't get up in the morning at all.

搬家		bānjiā	v.o.	to move households
搬		bān	v.	to move
校外		xiàowài	n.	off campus
房间	房間	fángjiān	n.	room
厕所	廁所	cèsuǒ	n.	restroom, bathroom
浴室		yùshì	n.	shower room

第二十七课 我得搬家

（A——小英，B——妈妈）

A：妈，住在宿舍里太不方便了，我想搬到校外去住。

B：宿舍离教室和图书馆都很近，你怎么说不方便呢？

A：房间里没有厕所，也没有浴室，每天早上都得等半天才能洗澡。我常常迟到，就是因为用厕所的人太多了。

B：那你早点儿起来，就不用等了。

A：我每天做作业做到一两点才睡觉，早上根本起不来。

半天	bàntiān	n.	a long while (literally "half day")
洗澡	xǐzǎo	v.o.	to take a shower
不用	búyòng	aux.	not necessary, no need to

B: Nà nǐ jiù zǎodiǎnr shuì ba.

A: Zǎodiǎnr shuì jiù zuòbuwán zuòyè le.

B: Wǒ shàngcì qù kànnǐ, juéde nǐde sùshè tǐnghǎo de. Fángjiān yòudà yòuliàng, chuáng hé zhuōyǐ yě dōu hěn shūfu. Xǐzǎo hé shàng cèsuǒ shì xiǎo wèntí.

A: Sùshè lǐ méiyǒu chúfáng yě hěn bù fāngbiàn.

B: Nǐ búshì zài shítáng chīfàn ma? Wèishénme hái yào chúfáng ne?

A: Shítáng de fàn nánchī jíle, wǒ chángcháng chībúxiàqù. Wǒ nìngkě zìjǐ zuòfàn, yě bùxiǎng qù shítáng. Méiyǒu chúfáng, shénme dōu zuòbuliǎo.

B: Sùshè fùjìn búshì yǒu jiā xiǎo fànguǎnr ma? Bùxiǎng zài shítáng chīfàn, jiù qù nàr chī ba.

A: Nèijiā fànguǎnr xiǎo shì xiǎo, kěshì bìng bù piányi. Wǒ chībuqǐ.

B: In that case, go to bed earlier.

A: If I sleep earlier, I can't finish my homework.

B: Last time I went to see you, I thought your dorm was quite nice. Your room is big and bright, and the bed, the desk, and the chairs are also comfortable. Taking a shower and using the bathroom are small problems.

A: It is also inconvenient that there is no kitchen in the dorm.

B: Don't you eat at the dinning hall? Why do you need a kitchen?

A: The dining hall's food is extremely bad, and I often can't swallow it. I would rather cook by myself than go to the dining hall. Without a kitchen, I cannot make anything.

B: Isn't there a small restaurant close to the dorm? If you don't want to eat at the dinning hall, then go eat there.

A: Although it is small, that restaurant is actually not cheap. I can't afford to eat there.

B：那你就早点儿睡吧。

A：早点儿睡就做不完作业了。

B：我上次去看你，觉得你的宿舍挺好的。房间又大又亮，床和桌椅也都很舒服。洗澡和上厕所是小问题。

A：宿舍里没有厨房也很不方便。

B：你不是在食堂吃饭吗？为什么还要厨房呢？

A：食堂的饭难吃极了，我常常吃不下去。我宁可自己做饭，也不想去食堂。没有厨房，什么都做不了。

B：宿舍附近不是有家小饭馆儿吗？不想在食堂吃饭，就去那儿吃吧。

A：那家饭馆儿小是小，可是并不便宜。我吃不起。

亮		liàng	adj.	bright
桌椅		zhuōyǐ	n.	desk and chair (the fusion form for 桌子椅子)
厨房	廚房	chúfáng	n.	kitchen
食堂		shítáng	n.	dining hall
难吃	難吃	nánchī	adj.	unsavory (food)
宁可	寧可	nìngkě	adv.	would rather
吃不起		chībuqǐ	v.c.	cannot afford eating

B: Nà jiù duō mǎi diǎnr fāngbiàn miàn, è le, jiù pào fāngbiàn miàn chī ba.

A: Zhù zài sùshè lǐ, chúle cèsuǒ hé chúfáng bù fāngbiàn yǐwài, háiyǒu yíjiànshì, zuì ràng wǒ shòubuliǎo.

B: Shénme shì a?

A: Wǒ tóngwū de nán péngyou měitiān wǎnshàng dōu lái wǒmen sùshè hé tā liáotiānr, yǒushíhòu liáo dào yì liǎng diǎn, ràng wǒ méi bànfa kànshū. Yǒu jǐtiān wǎnshàng tā hái shuì zài wǒmen wūzi lǐ, ràng wǒ juéde fēicháng bù fāngbiàn.

B: Tīng nǐ zhème shuō, nǐ shì děi bānjiā le.

B: In that case, buy some more instant noodles. If you are hungry, make some instant noodles to eat.

A: Besides the inconvenience with the restroom and kitchen, there is another thing that makes living in the dorm the most unbearable for me.

B: What is the matter?

A: My roommate's boyfriend comes to our dorm every night to chat with her. Sometimes they talk till one or two that I have no way to study. He has even slept in our room for several nights. This was very inconvenient for me.

B: From what you have said, you indeed have to move.

B：那就多买点儿方便面，饿了，就泡方便面吃吧。

A：住在宿舍里，除了厕所和厨房不方便以外，还有一件事，最让我受不了。

B：什么事啊？

A：我同屋的男朋友每天晚上都来我们宿舍和她聊天，有时候聊到一两点，让我没办法看书。有几天晚上，他还睡在我们屋子里，让我觉得非常不方便。

B：听你这么说，你是得搬家了。

方便面	方便麵	fāngbiàn miàn	n.	instant noodles
泡		pào	v.	to steep something in hot water
受不了		shòubuliǎo	v.c.	cannot put up with, unbearable

语法 Grammar Notes

1. 不用 + v. (do not need to; it is not necessary that …)

To express "have to, must," use 得 + V., or 一定得 + V. However, 得 does not have a negative form. To express "do not have to," one uses 不用.

▶ 那你早点儿起来，就不用等了。
   If you get up earlier, then you do not need to wait.

我坐公共汽车去学校，你不用开车送我。
I will take the bus to school. You do not need to give me a ride.

2. Verb + Complement

In this lesson, there are several verb complements that go with specific verbs and have different implications. All the verb complements below are given in their positive and negative potential forms.

(1) 来 as complement: 起得来/起不来　　to be able to get up

▶ 我每天做作业做到一两点才睡，早上根本起不来。
   I do my homework and do not sleep until one or two o'clock every night. I cannot get up in the morning at all.

(2) 了 (pronounced as "liǎo") as complement: 受得了/受不了 to be able to put up with …

了 emphasizes the successful completion of an action. Besides 受得了, there are also 做得了 (be able to do), 吃得了 (be able to eat up), 喝得了 (be able to drink up), 用得了 (be able to use up).

我睡觉的时候，我的同屋总是打电话，真让人受不了。
My roommate always makes calls when I sleep. This is indeed unbearable.

(3) 下去 as a complement: 吃得下去/吃不下去　to be able to swallow

下去 emphasizes the direction of going down. You may also say 喝得下去/喝不下去 (to be able to drink)

▶ 食堂的饭难吃极了，我常常吃不下去。
   The food at the dining hall is so bad, I often cannot swallow it.

(4) 起 as a complement: 吃得起/吃不起

This emphasizes the affordability of the object. There are also 买得起/买不起 (to afford/to be able to buy) 用得起/用不起 (to afford to use)

▶ 那家小饭馆儿并不便宜，我吃不起。
That little restaurant is actually not cheap. I cannot afford to eat there.

3. 宁可 Verb 1, 也不 Verb 2 (would rather V.1 than V.2)

This sentence pattern expresses the speaker's preference and choice after comparison of two imperfect alternatives or finding the lesser of the two evils. The phrase with 宁可 is the action chosen.

▶ 食堂的饭难吃极了，我宁可自己做饭，也不想去食堂。
The food at the dining hall is very bad. I would rather cook by myself than go to the dining hall.

我宁可死，也不跟他结婚。
I would rather die than marry him.

4. Review: 除了……（以外） (besides, except)

除了 corresponds to two meanings in English.

(1) "Besides, in addition to" if a positive statement follows.

▶ 除了厕所不方便以外，还有一件事，最让我受不了。
Besides the inconvenience of the restroom, there is still another thing that is the most unbearable for me.

还 (still) or 也 (also) is a marker that 除了 in this sentence means "in addition to" or "besides." The element after 除了 can be a verb phrase as in the above example; it can also be a noun. 以外 is optional; you may drop 以外.

除了茶，她也喜欢喝咖啡。
Besides tea, she also likes to drink coffee.

(2) Except, except for

除了跑步以外，别的运动他都不喜欢。
Except jogging, he doesn't like any other sports.

5. 是 + v./adj.

This pattern seems to contradict the basic rule of Chinese that you learned earlier, that is, that the verb 是 does not coexist with other verbs or adjectives. To translate "She is beautiful" into Chinese:

她很漂亮。 (correct)

她是漂亮。 (wrong; this is the most common mistake)

However, in some special contexts, 她是漂亮 is also correct. When one confirms an opinion or statement, 是 can be added:

她是(很)漂亮。

The above sentence would mean "Yes, she is indeed beautiful." In this case, 是 is used as an emphatic element and precedes verbs (except 是 itself) and adjectives. It can be translated as "indeed" or "certainly."

▶ 听你这么说，你是得搬家了。

From what you said, you indeed have to move.

昨天晚上是下雨了。

It did rain last night.

Traditional Character Text

我得搬家

（A——小英，B——媽媽）

A：媽，住在宿舍裏太不方便了，我想搬到校外去住。

B：宿舍離教室和圖書館都很近，你怎麼説不方便呢？

A：房間裏沒有廁所，也沒有浴室，每天早上都得等半天才能洗澡。我常常遲到，就是因為用廁所的人太多了。

B：那你早點兒起來，就不用等了。

A：我每天做作業做到一兩點才睡覺，早上根本起不來。

B：那你就早點兒睡吧。

A：早點兒睡就做不完作業了。

B：我上次去看你，覺得你的宿舍挺好的。房間又大又亮，床和桌椅也都很舒服。洗澡和上廁所是小問題。

A：宿舍裏沒有廚房也很不方便。

B：你不是在食堂吃飯嗎？為什麼還要廚房呢？

A：食堂的飯難吃極了，我常常吃不下去。我寧可自己做飯，也不想去食堂。沒有廚房，什麼都做不了。

B：宿舍附近不是有家小飯館兒嗎？不想在食堂吃飯，就去那兒吃吧。

A：那家飯館兒小是小，可是並不便宜。我吃不起。

B：那就多買點兒方便麵，餓了，就泡方便麵吃吧。

A：住在宿舍裏，除了廁所和廚房不方便以外，還有一件事，最讓我受不了。

B：什麼事啊？

A：我同屋的男朋友每天晚上都來我們宿舍和她聊天兒，有時候聊到一兩點，讓我沒辦法看書。有幾天晚上，他還睡在我們屋子裏，讓我覺得非常不方便。

B：聽你這麼説，你是得搬家了。

Pinyin Text

(A—Xiǎoyīng, B—Māma)

A: Mā, zhùzài xiàowài hái bùrú zhùzài sùshè lǐ ne, wǒ zhēn bùgāi bān chūlái.

B: Zěnme le? Búshì nǐ zìjǐ yào bān chūlái zhù de ma ?

A: Gēn wǒ zhùzài tóng yíge gōngyù lǐ de liǎngge nánshēng tàilǎnle! Tāmen cónglái bù dǎsǎo cèsuǒ, cèsuǒ lǐ yòu zāng yòu chòu, jiǎnzhí jìnbúqù!

B: Shénme! Nǐ gēn nánshēng zhù zài yíge gōngyù lǐ a?

A: Shì a, xuéxiào lǐ yě shì nánnǚshēng zhù zài yíge sùshè lǐ a. Zhè yǒu shénme bùtóng ne?

B: Zhèige … zhèige … , háishì yǒuxiē bùtóng de. Sùshè lǐ rén duō. …

English Translation

(A—Xiaoying, B—Mother)

A: Mom, living off campus is not even as good as living in the dorm. I really should not have moved out.

B: What happened? Wasn't it you yourself who wanted to move out?

A: The two guys who are sharing the apartment with me are extremely lazy! They never clean the bathroom. It is dirty and stinky, and you simply cannot go in.

B: What? You are sharing an apartment with guys?

A: Yes. Guys and girls live together in the university dorms too. What's the difference?

B: This … this … is still a little different. There are more people in the dorms. …

第二十八课 住在校外不如住在宿舍

（A——小英，B——妈妈）

A：妈，住在校外还不如住在宿舍里呢，我真不该搬出来。

B：怎么了？不是你自己要搬出来住的吗？

A：跟我住在同一个公寓里的两个男生太懒了！他们从来不打扫厕所，厕所里又脏又臭，简直进不去！

B：什么！你跟男生住在一个公寓里啊？

A：是啊，学校里也是男女生住在一个宿舍里啊。这有什么不同呢？

B：这个……这个……，还是有些不同的，宿舍里人多……

公寓		gōngyù	n.	apartment
男生		nánshēng	n.	male student
打扫	打掃	dǎsǎo	v.	to clean (a room)
脏	髒	zāng	adj.	dirty
臭		chòu	adj.	stinky, smelly
简直	簡直	jiǎnzhí	adv.	simply
女生		nǚshēng	n.	female student

A: Mā, wǒ bù gāoxìng búshì yīnwèi tāmen shì nánshēng, érshì yīnwèi tāmen tàilǎnle. Kètīng, fàntīng, wòshì, dàochù dōu shì tāmen de zāng yīfu. Yǒushíhou wǒ xiǎng kànyíxià diànshì, lián zuò de dìfang dōu méiyǒu.

A: Mom, I'm unhappy not because they are guys, but because they are too lazy. In the living room, dining room, and bedroom, their dirty clothes are everywhere. Sometimes when I want to watch TV, there isn't even a place to sit.

B: Nǐ gēn tāmen shuōguo zhèige wèntí ma?

B: Have you talked with them about this problem?

A: Shuōguo jǐ bǎi cì le, yìdiǎnr yòng dōu méiyǒu. Tāmen chī wán fàn yě bù xǐwǎn. Pánzi, bēizi, dāozi, chāzi dōu duī zài nàr. Běnlái yǐwéi bāndào xiàowài kěyǐ zìjǐ zuòfàn, xiànzài lián pào bēi chá dōu hěnnán.

A: I have talked about it hundreds of times, but it's not useful at all. They don't wash the dishes after dinner either. Plates, cups, knives, and forks are all piled up there. I had thought if I moved off campus, I could cook for myself, but now it's hard even to make a cup of tea.

B: Nà zěnme bàn?

B: Then what are you going to do?

客厅	客廳	kètīng	n.	living room
饭厅	飯廳	fàntīng	n.	dining room
卧室	卧室	wòshì	n.	bedroom
一下		yíxià	m.w.	measure word for verbs to show the briefness of the action
电视	電視	diànshì	n.	TV, TV programs

A：妈，我不高兴不是因为他们是男生，而是因为他们太懒了。客厅、饭厅、卧室，到处都是他们的脏衣服。有时候我想看一下电视，连坐的地方都没有。

B：你跟他们说过这个问题吗？

A：说过几百次了，一点儿用都没有。他们吃完饭也不洗碗。盘子、杯子、刀子、叉子都堆在那儿。本来以为搬到校外，可以自己做饭，现在连泡杯茶都很难。

B：那怎么办？

没有用		méiyǒuyòng	phrase	useless
洗碗		xǐwǎn	v.o.	to wash dish
盘子	盤子	pánzi	n.	plate
堆		duī	v.	to pile up

A: Tāmen lǎn shì lǎn, zāng shì zāng, kěshì duì wǒ dōu tǐnghǎode. Dàwěi shàngge zhōumò qǐng wǒ zài fùjìn de Zhōngguó fànguǎnr chīle yídùn wǎnfàn. Tā yǒu chē, xiàge xīngqī hái yào dài wǒ qù Niǔyuē wánr ne.

B: Dàwěi bǐ nǐ dà, háishì bǐ nǐ xiǎo a? Tā shì xué shénme de? Jiā zài nǎr? Bàba shì zuò shénme de?

A: Mā, nǐ zěnme xiàng jǐngchá yíyàng wèn wèntí a? Tā bǐ wǒ dà yí suì, shì xué jīngjì de, jiā zài Fèichéng. Tā bàba shì zuò shénme de, wǒ yě bù zhīdào.

B: Zhème zhòngyào de wèntí nǐ zěnme lián wèn dōu bú wèn ne?

A: Mā, wǒ shì gēn Dàwěi jiāo péngyou, búshì gēn tā bàba jiāo péngyou.

B: Nǐmen de gōngyù lǐ yígòng zhùle jǐge rén?

A: Lián wǒ yígòng zhùle sìge rén.

B: Chúle nǐ hé Dàwěi, háiyǒu shéi a?

A: Háiyǒu Xiǎo Dīng hé Sū Sān.

A: Admittedly, they are lazy and dirty, but they both are nice to me. David invited me to dinner in a restaurant nearby last weekend. He has a car and is going to drive me to New York to have fun next week.

B: Is David older or younger than you? What does he study? Where is his home? What does his father do?

A: Mom, why are you asking questions like a cop? He's a year older than me, he studies economics, his home is in Philadelphia, and as for what his father does, I don't know either.

B: Why wouldn't you ask an important question like that?

A: Mom, I'm making friends with David, not with his father.

B: How many people are there all together living in your apartment?

A: There are all together four people including me.

B: Besides you and David, who else?

A: There are also Xiao Ding and Susan.

大伟	大偉	Dàwěi	personal name	David
顿	頓	dùn	m.w.	measure word for meals
玩(儿)		wán(r)	v.	to play, to have fun

A：他们懒是懒，脏是脏，可是对我都挺好的。大伟上个周末请我在附近的中国饭馆儿吃了一顿晚饭。他有车，下个星期还要带我去纽约玩儿呢。

B：大伟比你大，还是比你小啊？他是学什么的？家在哪儿？爸爸是做什么的？

A：妈，你怎么像警察一样问问题啊？他比我大一岁，是学经济的，家在费城。他爸爸是做什么的，我也不知道。

B：这么重要的问题你怎么连问都不问呢？

A：妈，我是跟大伟交朋友，不是跟他爸爸交朋友。

B：你们的公寓里一共住了几个人？

A：连我一共住了4个人。

B：除了你和大伟，还有谁啊？

A：还有小丁和苏三。

经济	經濟	jīngjì	n.	economics
费城	費城	Fèichéng	proper n.	Philadelphia
一共		yígòng	adv.	all together, in total
苏	蘇	Sū	n.	Su, a Chinese last name
苏三	蘇三	Sū Sān	personal name	Susan

语法 Grammar Notes

1. 不是……而是…… (not … , but …)

This structure negates one possibility (the choice after 不是), which the audience assumes, and confirms the other (the choice after 而是), and thus it corrects the prior incorrect impression. It marks a strong contrast between the two and emphasizes the one that is chosen.

> 她的爸爸不是老师，而是警察。
> Her father is not a teacher, but a policeman.

> 我们不是明天去纽约，而是下个周末。
> It is not tomorrow, but next weekend that we will go to New York.

This structure is often used to provide reasons.

> **Statement,** 不是因为……，而是因为……
> Not because … but because …

> ▶ 我不高兴，不是因为他们是男生，而是因为他们太懒了。
> I'm unhappy not because they are guys, but because they are too lazy.

2. Review: 连……都…… (even)

(1) To emphasize the subject, use this pattern: 连 subject 都 V. (O.).

> 连老师都不会写这个字。
> Even the teacher doesn't know how to write this character.

(2) To emphasize the object, use this pattern: Subject 连 object 都 V.

> ▶ 有时候我想看一下电视，连坐的地方也没有。
> Sometimes I want to watch some TV, but there is not even a place to sit.

(3) To emphasize the verb, use this pattern: Object + subject 连 V.都不/没 V.

Note that in this pattern, the sentence is usually negative, and the verb must be repeated. If the verb takes an object, the object is usually placed at the beginning of the sentence.

> ▶ 这么重要的问题，你怎么连问都不问呢？
> How could you even fail to ask such an important question?

3. 连 A 一共 (+ V.) + amount (including A, there are all together …)

▶ 连我一共住了4个人.

   Including me, there are all together four people living here.

   连这双球鞋，我一共有5双鞋。

   Including this pair of sneakers, I have five pairs of shoes all together.

4. 一点儿 noun 都不／没 + V. (do not have even a little bit of …)

This is an emphatic form for a negative sentence.

The expression in the text 一点用都没有 originates from the phrase 有用 (useful), the negative of which is 没有用 (not useful). 一点用都没有 is an emphatic form of the negative. 有用, functioning as an adjective, is a "verb + object" construction, and literally means "to have some use."

▶ 说过几百次了，一点用都没有。

   I have talked about it hundreds of times, but all in vain (it has no use at all).

   我一点儿咖啡都不喝。

   I do not drink coffee at all.

   一点意思都没有。

   Not interesting at all. (See Lesson 14, note 7.)

   For countable nouns: 一 + m.w. + noun + 都不／没 + V.

   他一个朋友都没有。

   He does not even have one friend.

5. 对 (to treat)

In the text, 对 is used as a verb, meaning "to treat." 对 is often followed by a description in the pattern "A 对 B + descriptive word," to show A's attitude toward B.

▶ 他们懒是懒，脏是脏，可是对我都挺好的。

   Admittedly, they are lazy and dirty, but they both are nice to me.

   他们对人很不客气。

   They treat people impolitely.

6. 是……的

(1) To talk about a profession

▶A: 他爸爸是做什么的？ What does his father do?
B: 他爸爸是警察。 His father is a policeman.

(2) To talk about a specialty or major

▶A: 他是学什么的？ What does he study? (What is his major?)
B: 他是学经济的。 He is an economics major.

Traditional Character Text

住在校外不如住在宿舍

(A——小英，B——媽媽)

A：媽，住在校外還不如住在宿舍裏呢，我真不該搬出來。

B：怎麼了？不是你自己要搬出來住的嗎？

A：跟我住在同一個公寓裏的兩個男生太懶了！他們從來不打掃廁所，廁所裏又髒又臭，簡直進不去！

B：什麼！你跟男生住在一個公寓裏啊？

A：是啊，學校裏也是男女生住在一個宿舍裏啊，這有什麼不同呢？

B：這個……這個……還是有些不同的，宿舍裏人多……

A：媽，我不高興不是因為他們是男生，而是因為他們太懶了。客廳、飯廳、臥室，到處都是他們的髒衣服。有時候我想看一下電視，連坐的地方都沒有。

B：你跟他們說過這個問題嗎？

A：說過幾百次了，一點兒用都沒有。他們吃完飯也不洗碗。盤子、杯子、刀子、叉子都堆在那兒。本來以為搬到校外，可以自己做飯，現在連泡杯茶都很難。

B：那怎麼辦呢？

A：他們懶是懶，髒是髒，可是對我都挺好的。大偉上個週末請我在附近的中國飯館吃了一頓晚飯。他有車，下個星期還要帶我去紐約玩兒呢。

B：大偉比你大，還是比你小啊？他是學什麼的？家在哪兒？爸爸是做什麼的？

A：媽，你怎麼像警察一樣問問題啊？他比我大一歲，是學經濟的，家在費城。他爸爸是做什麼的，我也不知道。

B：這麼重要的問題你怎麼連問都不問呢？

A：媽，我是跟大偉交朋友，不是跟他爸爸交朋友。

B：你們的公寓裏一共住了幾個人？

A：連我一共住了4個人。

B：除了你和大偉，還有誰啊？

A：還有小丁和蘇三。

29 Xiǎo Dīng hé Sū Sān (Xiao Ding and Susan)

Pinyin Text

(A—Māma, B—Xiǎoyīng)

A: Xiǎo Dīng shì nánde háishì nǔde a?

B: Xiǎo Dīng shì nánde.

A: Yuánlái nǐmen liǎngnán liǎngnǔ zhù yíge gōngyù.

B: Shì a, wǒmen dōushì hǎo péngyou, yě hěn tándelái, suǒyǐ zhù zài yìqǐ.

A: Xiǎo Dīng shì Měiguó rén ma?

B: Xiǎo Dīng de bàba shì Měiguó rén, māma shì Zhōngguó rén. Tā kànqǐlái yǒudiǎnr xiàng Měiguó rén, yě yǒudiǎnr xiàng Zhōngguó rén. Tā tóufa shì hēide, kěshì yǎnjīng shì lánde, bízi yǒudiǎnr dà, gèzi bǐjiào gāo, shì xuéxiào lánqiú duì de duìyuán. Hěnduō nǔshēng dōu xǐhuān tā.

English Translation

(A—Mother, B—Xiaoying)

A: Is Xiao Ding male or female?

B: Xiao Ding is male.

A: Actually you two girls are sharing the apartment with two guys.

B: Yes, we are all good friends, and we get along well, so we live together.

A: Is Xiao Ding American?

B: Xiao Ding's father is American, and his mother is Chinese. He looks a bit like an American, and a bit like a Chinese person too. His hair is black, but his eyes are blue; his nose is a little large, and he is quite tall. He is a member of the school's basketball team. Many girls like him.

第二十九课 小丁和苏三

（A——妈妈，B——小英）

A：小丁是男的还是女的啊？

B：小丁是男的。

A：原来你们两男两女住一个公寓。

B：是啊，我们都是好朋友，也很谈得来，所以住在一起。

A：小丁是美国人吗？

B：小丁的爸爸是美国人，妈妈是中国人。他看起来有点儿像美国人，也有点儿像中国人。他头发是黑的，可是眼睛是蓝的，鼻子有点儿大，个子比较高，是学校篮球队的队员。很多女生都喜欢他。

原来	原來	yuánlái	adv.	as it turns out …
篮球	籃球	lánqiú	n.	basketball
队	隊	duì	n.	team
队员	隊員	duìyuán	n.	team member

A: Sū Sān shì cóng nǎr láide a?

B: Sū Sān shì Rìběn rén. Tā bàba zài xuéxiào fùjìn kāile yìjiā Rìběn fànguǎnr, jiālǐ chángcháng gěi tā sòng chīde dōngxi. Wǒ zuì xǐhuān chī tā bàba zuòde shēngyúpiàn, yòu xīnxiān yòu hǎochī.

A: Sū Sān shì jǐ niánjí de xuéshēng?

B: Tā shì sān niánjí de xuéshēng, zhuānyè shì Dōngyà yánjiū. Tā yòu cōngming yòu piàoliang, búdàn huì shuō Rìwén, érqiě huì shuō Zhōngwén. Tā rénhǎo, xuéxí hǎo, yě hěn xǐhuān yùndòng. Chángcháng yǒu nánshēng dǎ diànhuà gěitā.

A: Xiǎo Dīng búshì tāde nán péngyou ma?

B: Hěnduō nánshēng suīrán zhīdào tā yǒu nán péngyou, kěshì hái tiāntiān gěi tā dǎ diànhuà. Tā yě hěn xǐhuān gēn biéde nánshēng liáotiānr, hē kāfēi shénme de. Wúlùn shéi gěi tā dǎ diànhuà, tā dōu yǒushuō yǒuxiào. Xiǎo Dīng chángcháng yīnwèi zhèige gēn tā chǎojià.

A: Where is Susan from？

B: Susan is Japanese. Her father runs a Japanese restaurant near school, and her family often sends her food. I like the sashimi her father makes the most. It's fresh and tasty.

A: What grade is Susan in?

B: She is a junior majoring in East Asian Studies. She is both smart and pretty. She can speak not only Japanese, but also Chinese. She has a good personality, good grades, and she likes sports. There are often guys who call her.

A: Isn't Xiao Ding her boyfriend?

B: Although many guys know that she has a boyfriend, they still call her every day. She also likes to chat or have coffee with other guys. No matter who calls her, she answers the phone talking and laughing. Xiao Ding often quarrels with her because of this.

A：苏三是从哪儿来的啊？

B：苏三是日本人。她爸爸在学校附近开了一家日本饭馆儿，家里常常给她送吃的东西。我最喜欢吃她爸爸做的生鱼片，又新鲜又好吃。

A：苏三是几年级的学生？

B：她是三年级的学生，专业是东亚研究。她又聪明又漂亮，不但会说日文，而且会说中文。她人好，学习好，也很喜欢运动。常常有男生打电话给她。

A：小丁不是她的男朋友吗？

B：很多男生虽然知道她有男朋友，可是还天天给她打电话。她也很喜欢跟别的男生聊天，喝咖啡什么的。无论谁给她打电话，她都有说有笑。小丁常常因为这个跟她吵架。

开	開	kāi	v.	to run; to open (a store)
生		shēng	adj.	raw (meat, fish, etc.)
鱼片	魚片	yúpiàn	n.	fish fillet
生鱼片	生魚片	shēngyúpiàn	n.	sashimi
新鲜	新鮮	xīnxiān	adj.	fresh
专业	專業	zhuānyè	n.	major, specialty
研究		yánjiū	n./v.	research; to do research
什么的	什麼的	shénme de	phrase	… and so forth, etc.
吵架		chǎojià	v.o.	to argue, to quarrel

A: Sū Sān dàodǐ xǐ bù xǐhuān Xiǎo Dīng?

B: Wǒ juéde tā háishì tǐng xǐhuān Xiǎo Dīng de. Tāmen dǎsuàn xiàtiān yìqǐ qù Rìběn. Yìfāngmiàn xué Rìwén, yìfāngmiàn kànkan zài Rìběn de qīnqi péngyou. Tāmen yí fàng shǔjià jiù qù Rìběn.

A: Nǐmen de shēnghuó tǐng yǒu yìsi de. Wǒ hái yǐwéi nǐ bù xǐhuān bāndào xiàowài qù zhù ne. Xiànzài wǒ jiù fàngxīn le.

A: Does Susan like Xiao Ding at all?

B: I think that she still likes Xiao Ding a lot. They plan to go to Japan together in the summer. On one hand, they can learn Japanese, and on the other hand, they can visit relatives and friends in Japan. They will go to Japan as soon as summer break starts.

A: Your life is pretty interesting. I thought that you didn't like moving out and living off campus. Now I can rest assured.

A：苏三到底喜不喜欢小丁？

B：我觉得她还是挺喜欢小丁的。他们打算夏天一起去日本。一方面学日文，一方面看看在日本的亲戚朋友。他们一放暑假就去日本。

A：你们的生活挺有意思的。我还以为你不喜欢搬到校外去住呢。现在我就放心了。

到底		dàodǐ	adv.	to the end, what on earth …
打算		dǎsuàn	v.	to plan to do
一方面		yìfāngmiàn	conj.	on one hand, in one aspect
亲戚	親戚	qīnqi	n.	relatives
暑假		shǔjià	n.	summer break
放暑假		fàng shǔjià	v.o.	to have summer break
生活		shēnghuó	n.	life

语法 Grammar Notes

1. 原来

The adverb 原来 indicates a sudden realization or discovery of a new situation or the actual cause of the situation. It is often paired with a clause of 以为 (one thought) to mark a contrast between the prior impression and the newly discovered fact.

▶ 原来你们两男两女住一个公寓。

Actually you two girls are sharing the apartment with two guys.

原来你不喜欢大伟啊，我还以为你们在谈恋爱呢。

[I just realized that] you don't like David. I thought that you were dating him.

2. A 跟B 谈得来 (A gets along well with B)

谈 (v.) as in 谈话 means to talk. 谈得来 literally means that people have a lot to talk about or share many common topics. It's negative form is 谈不来.

▶ 我们都是好朋友，也很谈得来。

We are all good friends, and we get along well.

我跟我的同屋最谈得来。

I get along the best with my roommate.

3. 送

(1) To give as a gift:　送给 somebody something
　　　　　　　　　　　送 something 给 somebody
　　　　　　　　　　　给 somebody 送 something

我送给他一本书。

I gave him a book as a gift.

(2) To deliver, to bring:　送 something 给 somebody
　　　　　　　　　　　　给 somebody 送 something

▶ 家里常常给她送吃的东西。

Her family often sends her food.

(3) To escort, to accompany: 送 somebody 去 V./place
                                  把 somebody 送到 place

我送朋友去学校。
I accompanied my friend to the school.

4. 还

There are two instances of 还 in this text, and they have different usages.

(1) Still

▶ 很多男生虽然知道她有男朋友，可是还天天给她打电话。
   Although many guys know that she has a boyfriend, they still call her every day.

已经很晚了，他还在工作。
It was already very late. He was still working.

(2) To express surprise, contrary to one's expectation, often combined with 以为

Subject 还以为 + clause   (mistakenly thought …)

▶ 我还以为你不喜欢搬到校外去住呢。
   I thought you didn't like moving out and living off campus.

听说你病了，我还以为你今天不来了。
I heard that you were sick. I thought you would not come today.

5. A, B, C 什么的

This structure is used to provide a list of items. 什么的 is placed at the end of the list, meaning "and so forth."

▶ 她也喜欢跟别的男生喝咖啡，聊天儿什么的。
   She also likes having coffee and chatting with other guys, and so on.

我昨天买了苹果、桔子、香蕉什么的。
Yesterday I bought apples, oranges, bananas, etc.

6. 到底 (adv.) (on earth, after all)

到底 is used before a question to express the eagerness of the inquirer to know the answer.

> 到底 + V.不V.
> 到底 + (是) A还是B
> 到底 + question word

The response to each of these questions must not include 到底, which can be used only in a question, not in a statement.

▶ 苏三到底喜不喜欢小丁啊？
Does Susan like Xiao Ding or not?

你到底想吃牛肉还是猪肉？
Do you want to have beef or pork?

你到底喜欢什么运动？
What sports do you like?

7. 一方面 (on one hand, in one aspect)

一方面……一方面……can be used to show different aspects of a situation.

▶ 一方面学日文，一方面看看在日本的亲戚朋友。
On one hand, they study Japanese; and on the other hand, they see relatives and friends in Japan.

骑自行车去学校，一方面可以锻炼身体，一方面也很方便，不用找停车的地方。
Going to school by bike, on one hand it is good exercise, on the other hand, it is very convenient. You don't have to look for parking.

Traditional Character Text

小丁和蘇三

（A——媽媽，B——小英）

A：小丁是男的還是女的啊？

B：小丁是男的。

A：原來你們兩男兩女住一個公寓。

B：是啊，我們都是好朋友，也很談得來，所以住在一起。

A：小丁是美國人嗎？

B：小丁的爸爸是美國人，媽媽是中國人。他看起來有點兒像美國人，也有點兒像中國人。他頭髮是黑的，可是眼睛是藍的，鼻子有點兒大，個子比較高，是學校籃球隊的隊員。很多女生都喜歡他。

A：蘇三是從哪兒來的啊？

B：蘇三是日本人。她爸爸在學校附近開了一家日本飯館兒，家裏常常給她送吃的東西。我最喜歡吃她爸爸做的生魚片，又新鮮又好吃。

A：蘇三是幾年級的學生啊？

B：她是三年級的學生，專業是東亞研究。她又聰明又漂亮，不但會說日文，而且會說中文。她人好，學習好，也很喜歡運動。常常有男生打電話給她。

A：小丁不是她的男朋友嗎？

B：很多男生雖然知道她有男朋友，可是還天天給她打電話。她也很喜歡跟別的男生聊天兒，喝咖啡什麼的。無論誰給她打電話，她都有説有笑。小丁常常因為這個跟她吵架。

A：蘇三到底喜不喜歡小丁？

B：我覺得她還是挺喜歡小丁的。他們打算夏天一起去日本。一方面學日文，一方面看看在日本的親戚朋友。他們一放暑假就去日本。

A：你們的生活挺有意思的。我還以為你不喜歡搬到校外去住呢。現在我就放心了。

30 Gěi Bàba Māma de Diànzǐ Yóujiàn
(An Email to Parents)

Pinyin Text

Bàba, Māma:

Nǐmen hǎo ma? Wǒ hěnxiǎng nǐmen.

Shíjiān guòde zhēnkuài, zhèige xuéqī mǎshàng jiùyào jiéshù le. Zhè yìnián wǒ xuǎn le hěnduō kè, wǒ zuì xǐhuān de shì Zhōngwén kè. Suīrán Zhōngwén kè hěnnán, érqiě yíge xīngqī děi shàng wǔjié kè, kěshì wǒ juéde hěn yǒuyòng.

Zài gāozhōng de shíhou, wǒ xuéle liǎngnián Fǎwén. Ná Fǎwén hé Zhōngwén bǐ, Fǎwén duì Měiguórén lái shuō, jiǎnzhí bùnéng suànshì wàiguóhuà. Fǎwén hé Yīngwén, búdàn yǒu hěnduō zì kànqǐlái chàbuduō, lián fāyīn yě méiyǒu hěndà de bùtóng.

English Translation

Dad and Mom:

How are you? I miss you very much.

Time is going by really quickly. This semester is almost over. This year, I've taken many classes, and my favorite is Chinese class. Although Chinese class is very difficult, and we also have to attend five class sessions every week, I think it's very useful.

In high school, I studied two years of French. When you compare French with Chinese, for Americans, French simply does not count as a foreign language. Not only do many words in French and English look similar, there isn't even a very big difference in the way they are pronounced.

邮件	郵件	yóujiàn	n.	mail
电子邮件	電子郵件	diànzǐyóujiàn	n.	e-mail
想		xiǎng	v.	to miss
过	過	guò	v.	to pass (time)

第三十课 给爸爸妈妈的电子邮件

爸爸、妈妈：

你们好吗？我很想你們。

时间过得真快，这个学期马上就要结束了。这一年我选了很多课，我最喜欢的是中文课。虽然中文课很难，而且一个星期得上5节课，可是我觉得很有用。

在高中的时候，我学了两年法文。拿法文和中文比，法文对美国人来说，简直不能算是外国话。法文和英文，不但有很多字看起来差不多，连发音也没有很大的不同。

高中		gāozhōng	n.	high school
法文		Fǎwén	n.	French (language)
算是		suànshì	v.	to be counted as
外国	外國	wàiguó	n.	foreign country
外国话	外國話	wàiguóhuà	n.	foreign language

Zhōngwén hé Yīngwén, wúlùn shì xiězì háishì fāyīn, dōu wánquán bù yíyàng. Xuéle Zhōngwén yǐhòu, wǒ kàndào le yíge xīn de wénhuà, xīn de shìjiè.

Jùshuō Zhōngguó xuéshēng cóng zhōngxué jiù kāishǐ xué Yīngwén, dànshì xué Zhōngwén de Měiguó xuéshēng què fēicháng shǎo. Měiguó rén rúguǒ zhēnxiǎng liǎojiě Zhōngguó, yīnggāi cóng xué Zhōngwén kāishǐ. Xuéxiào yǒu yíge Běijīng shǔqī Zhōngwén péixùnbān, wǒ hěnxiǎng cānjiā. Xīwàng nǐmen zhīchí wǒ.

Zhù bàba māma shēntǐ jiànkāng.

Xiǎoyīng

__nián__yuè__rì

No matter whether considering writing or pronunciation, Chinese and English are completely different. After having studied Chinese, I am able to see a new culture and a new world.

It is said that students in China start learning English as early as middle school. However, very few American students take Chinese. If Americans really want to understand China, they should start by studying Chinese. My school has a Beijing summer Chinese language program, and I really want to attend. I hope you will support me.

Wish you good health!

Xiaoying

yy/mm/dd

文化		wénhuà	n.	culture
世界		shìjiè	n.	world
中学	中學	zhōngxué	n.	middle school

中文和英文，无论是写字还是发音，都完全不一样。学了中文以后，我看到了一个新的文化，新的世界。

据说中国学生从中学就开始学英文，但是学中文的美国学生却非常少。美国人如果真想了解中国，应该从学中文开始。学校有一个北京暑期中文培训班，我很想参加。希望你们支持我。

祝爸爸妈妈身体健康！

小英

一年一月一日

如果		rúguǒ	conj.	if
了解		liǎojiě	v.	to understand, to comprehend
暑期		shǔqī	n.	the term of summer break
培训	培訓	péixùn	v./n.	to train; training
班		bān	n.	class
培训班	培訓班	péixùnbān	n.	training class
支持		zhīchí	v.	to support, to stand by
祝		zhù	v.	wish (used in greetings)

语法 Grammar Notes

1. Subject 就要 V.P. 了 (... is about to ...)

就 here means sooner than expected. 要……了 indicates that something is about to happen. Either 就 or 要 can be omitted in this pattern.

▶ 这个学期马上就要结束了。
This semester is about to end.

晚饭就要吃完了，我的朋友还没来。
The dinner is about to finish, but my friend has not come yet.

2. V. (了) Time Duration (的) + Object (to do something for (amount of time))

▶ 在高中的时候，我学了两年法文。
In high school, I studied two years of French.

我每天看一个小时的电视。
I watch TV for an hour every day.

This pattern is interchangeable with "V. (object + V.) (了) time duration." The above two examples can be rewritten as,

在高中的时候，我学法文学了两年。
我每天看电视看一个小时。

3. 拿 A 跟 B 比，…… (comparing A with B, ...)

▶ 拿法文和中文比，法文简直不能算是外国话。
When you compare French with Chinese, French simply cannot be considered a foreign language.

拿大学的课跟中学的比，大学的课比中学的难多了。
Comparing the classes in college with the ones in middle school, the classes in college are a lot more difficult.

4. Review: 对 somebody 来说 (for somebody, as far as somebody is concerned)

▶ 对美国人来说，法文简直不能算是外国话。
For Americans, French simply cannot count as a foreign language.

对一年级的中文学生来说，上课的时候完全不用英文很难。
For a first-year student of Chinese, it is difficult to completely not use English in class.

5. Review: 简直…… (simply)

This adverb is used to exaggerate or to emphasize.

It often goes before 不能, 没办法, 太……了 or the potential verb complement.

今天太热了，我简直没办法睡觉。
It is really hot today. There is simply no way for me to sleep.

那家饭馆儿的饭太难吃了，我简直吃不下去。
The food at that restaurant is so bad that I simply can't eat it.

6. 如果……, subject 就…… (If …)

如果 is interchangeable with 要是. 要是 is more colloquial.

▶ 美国人如果真想了解中国，应该从学中文开始。
If Americans really want to understand China, they should start by studying Chinese.

如果你想参加大学篮球队，你得多练习。
If you want to join the university basketball team, you have to practice more.

7. 从……开始 (start from …)

▶ 中国学生都从中学就开始学英文。
Students in China start learning English as early as middle school.

如果你想减肥，应该从不喝饮料开始。
If you want to lose weight, you should start by not drinking soft drinks.

8. Review

……, (但是/可是/不过) subject 却……

The adverb 却 is placed after the subject. It is often used with 但是/可是/不过.

▶ 中国学生从中学就开始学英文，但是学中文的美国学生却很少。
Students in China start learning English as early as middle school, but there are very few American students who study Chinese.

他的朋友都说他的衣服很奇怪，他自己却不觉得。
His friends all said that his clothes were strange, but he did not think so.

Traditional Character Text

給爸爸媽媽的電子郵件

爸爸、媽媽：

你們好嗎？我很想你們。

時間過得真快，這個學期馬上就要結束了。這一年我選了很多課，我最喜歡的是中文課。雖然中文課很難，而且一個星期得上五節課，可是我覺得很有用。

在高中的時候，我學了兩年法文。拿法文和中文比，法文對美國人來說，簡直不能算是外國話，法文和英文，不但有很多字看起來差不多，連發音也沒有很大的不同。中文和英文，無論是寫字還是發音，都完全不一樣。學了中文以後，我看到了一個新的文化，新的世界。

據說中國學生從中學就開始學英文，但是學中文的美國學生卻非常少。美國人如果真想瞭解中國，應該從學中文開始。學校有一個北京暑期中文培訓班，我很想參加。希望你們支持我。

祝爸爸媽媽身體健康！

小英

一年一月一日

PINYIN INDEX

The numbers following each entry indicate the lesson(s) (L.) and the page(s) (p.) where it appears.

ENGLISH INDEX

The numbers following each entry indicate the lesson(s) (L.) and the page(s) (p.) where it appears.